THE BOOK OF

# CHILDREN'S
# PARTY CAKES

THE BOOK OF

# CHILDREN'S PARTY CAKES

ANN NICOL

Photographed by
KARL ADAMSON

a Salamander book
Published by Salamander Books Limited
LONDON

Published by Salamander Books Limited
129-137 York Way, London N7 9LG, United Kingdom

9 8 7 6 5 4 3 2 1

© Salamander Books Ltd 1994

ISBN 0-86101-737-4

Managing Editor: Felicity Jackson
Art Director: Roger Daniels
Photography: Karl Adamson
Home Economist: Ann Nicol, assisted by Catherine Atkinson
Typeset by: Pearl Graphics, Hemel Hempstead
Colour separation by: Scantrans Pte. Ltd, Singapore
Printed in Belgium by Proost International Book Production

ACKNOWLEDGEMENTS

Regalice ready-to-roll sugarpaste icing supplied for
all photography by J. F. Renshaw Ltd.
Cake colourings and specialist decorating equipment:
Squires Kitchen Sugarcraft, 3 Waverley Lane,
Farnham, Surrey, GU9 8BB. Tel: 0252 711749.

**Notes:**
All spoon measurements are level.
1 teaspoon = 5 ml spoon.
1 tablespoon = 15 ml spoon.

# CONTENTS

COMPANION VOLUMES OF INTEREST:

The Book of SOUPS
The Book of COCKTAILS
The Book of CHOCOLATES & PETITS FOURS
The Book of HORS D'OEUVRES
The Book of GARNISHES
The Book of BREAKFASTS & BRUNCHES
The Book of PRESERVES
The Book of SAUCES
The Book of DESSERTS
The Book of ICE CREAMS & SORBETS
The Book of GIFTS FROM THE PANTRY
The Book of PASTA
The Book of HOT & SPICY NIBBLES-DIPS-DISHES
The Book of CRÊPES & OMELETTES
The Book of FONDUES
The Book of CHRISTMAS FOODS
The Book of BISCUITS
The Book of CHEESECAKES
The Book of CURRIES & INDIAN FOODS
The Book of PIZZAS & ITALIAN BREADS
The Book of SANDWICHES
The Book of SALADS
The Book of GRILLING & BARBECUES
The Book of DRESSINGS & MARINADES
The Book of CHINESE COOKING
The Book of CAKE DECORATING
The Book of MEXICAN FOODS
The Book of ANTIPASTI
The Book of THAI COOKING
The Book of CHILDREN'S FOODS
The Book of AFTERNOON TEA
The Book of GREEK COOKING
The Book of TAPAS AND SPANISH COOKING
The Book of CLAYPOT COOKING
The Book of VEGETARIAN COOKING
The Book of CHICKEN DISHES
The Book of WOK AND STIR-FRY DISHES
The Book of LIGHT DESSERTS
The Book of LIGHT SAUCES AND SALAD DRESSINGS
The Book of FISH AND SHELLFISH DISHES

# INTRODUCTION

Creating your own special cake for a child's party is great fun, and so much more satisfying than buying one from a shop. *The Book of Children's Party Cakes* gives you all the help you need to make that important birthday party really spectacular.

Even if you are a complete novice, you'll find the recipes easy to follow as the step-by-step photographs show you clearly how to make each cake, with full instructions for all the decorations.

The basic recipes for the cakes, icings and decorations are explained in detail at the front of the book. All the help you need to master techniques like icing and piping is given with step-by-step photographs, to help you achieve a really professional finish.

To make the cakes as easy as possible, some of the decorations are made from sweets and other confectionery that is widely available in supermarkets, so you don't need to find difficult ingredients. Templates and patterns to help you cut out special shapes are included at the back of the book.

The cake recipes start with simple faces for very young children, and work through a varied selection for all ages, finishing with dramatic creations like roller skates and a computer. You'll find yourself using this book again and again as your children grow up — so happy cake making!

# EQUIPMENT FOR PARTY CAKES

## CAKE BOARDS
A wide selection of shaped boards is available. As a general rule, use a board that is 5 cm (2 in) larger than the cake. For extra large cakes, you can always cover an upturned tea tray with foil.

## CAKE TINS
Basic tins are used for all the cakes in this book, as well as ovenproof pudding basins for round shapes. If you do a lot of baking, remember it is an investment to buy good quality tins.

## COCKTAIL STICKS
These are needed for adding colouring, securing some shapes, modelling and making frills.

## COLOURINGS
Use colourings in paste form for cake decorating. Liquid food colouring will cause sugarpaste icing to become limp and dull, and it can make butter cream too wet. Use paste colouring to colour sugarpaste, butter cream, royal icing and desiccated coconut. As it is concentrated, add a tiny amount only, with a cocktail stick.

## CRIMPERS
These are useful for giving simple patterns to borders and edges. They come in a range of different patterns.

## CUTTERS
An ordinary set of fluted round pastry cutters will help make frills, but look out for flower cutters for more advanced work.

## KNIFE
Always use a good sharp knife for cutting the cakes into shapes – don't use a breadknife. Sponge cakes are easier to cut if they are made the day before as they won't produce so many crumbs. Sponges also cut more easily if placed in the freezer for 20-30 minutes.

## MEASURING SPOONS
A set of metric or imperial measuring spoons is essential for accurate measurements. All spoon measurements in the book are level. Use metric or imperial – don't mix the two.

## PAINT BRUSHES
Buy one thin and one thick, good quality, sable artist's brush for painting directly onto sugarpaste icing.

## PALETTE KNIVES
A small palette knife is good for spreading icing onto sides and mixing in colours. A large one is useful for flat icing the top of a cake.

## PAPER
Strong greaseproof or non-stick silicone paper is needed for lining tins and making paper icing bags.

## PIPING NOZZLES
A wide range of fancy nozzles is available but only a plain No 1 nozzle and a small star are needed for the cakes in this book. It is worth buying more expensive ones with good, well-joined seams.

## ROLLING PINS
A long straight-ended rolling pin is needed for rolling out sugarpaste and almond paste. Large and small plastic rolling pins, specially made for use with sugarpaste icing, give much better results than wooden ones.

## SCISSORS
A large pair of scissors is needed for cutting greaseproof paper and small dressmaking scissors with fine points for snipping sugarpaste icing.

## SMOOTHER
A professional icing smoother makes all the difference and is essential for a smooth finish to sugarpaste and almond paste.

## SUGARPASTE
Ready-to-roll sugarpaste, or fondant, icing is the easiest form of icing to use as it can be rolled out, just like pastry, or easily moulded with the hands or tools. It is widely available in supermarkets and cake decorating shops. You can buy plain white or ready coloured varieties. The ready coloured, particularly black and darker colours, is useful for cakes which would require a lot of paste colouring to achieve the colour. Once opened, keep sugarpaste sealed in an airtight plastic bag in a cool place, or it will dry out.

## TURNTABLE
An icing turntable makes covering cakes much easier; alternatively, stand the cake on a plate on a large upturned pudding basin.

# BASIC RECIPES

## VICTORIA SPONGE

(See each individual recipe for tin sizes and baking times. If using fan assisted ovens, follow manufacturer's instructions and reduce or alter the baking times and temperatures accordingly.) See chart opposite for quantities of ingredients.

**Method**
Grease and line tin(s). Cream the butter and sugar together until light, fluffy and very pale. Beat in the beaten eggs gradually, adding a tablespoon of flour with each addition to stop the mixture from separating. Fold in the remaining flour, then add the hot water and fold until smooth. Bake at the temperature and for the time specified for each individual recipe until the cake is pale golden and springs back when touched. Leave in the tin for 3 minutes, then turn out onto a wire rack to cool.

## BUTTER CREAM

115 g (4 oz) unsalted butter
225 g (8 oz) icing sugar, sifted
2 tablespoons milk
2 drops vanilla essence
colouring of choice

In a bowl, beat the butter with half the icing sugar until smooth. Add remaining icing sugar with the milk, essence and colouring and beat until creamy.

*Makes 225 g (8 oz).*

**Note:** 115 g (4 oz) butter cream means made with 115 g (4 oz) butter.

**Variation:** Melt 55 g (2 oz) plain (dark) chocolate, cool, then beat in.

## AMERICAN SOFT ICING

175 g (6 oz) white vegetable fat
450 g (1 lb) sifted icing sugar
4 tablespoons tepid water
few drops of flavouring
colouring of choice

In a bowl, beat fat with half the icing sugar, then beat in remaining sugar with water, flavouring and colouring of your choice. Beat the icing until completely smooth. Use at room temperature.

*Makes 450 g (1 lb).*

**Note:** Quantities of icing specified in the recipes refer to the quantity of icing sugar used.

## ROYAL ICING

1 egg white
225 g (8 oz) sifted icing sugar
colouring (optional)

In a bowl, break up the egg white with a fork, then gradually beat in half the icing sugar. Beat in remaining icing sugar with colouring, if using. Beat for at least 5 minutes, otherwise the icing will be tough when cut. Leave in the bowl and cover with a damp cloth or a plastic lid to prevent it from drying out.

*Makes 225 g (8 oz).*

**Note:** Packs of royal icing mix are very handy for making small quantities. Use packet dried egg white if you don't want to use raw egg whites.

## APRICOT GLAZE

450 g (1 lb) apricot jam
3 tablespoons water

Put the jam and water into a saucepan and heat gently until the jam has melted. Boil rapidly for 1-2 minutes, then push through a sieve using a wooden spoon, to remove the pieces of fruit. Boil the strained jam for 1 minute, then pour into a clean, warm, dry jam jar and cool. Store in refrigerator for up to 2 months, and use as needed. Heat to melt before using.

**Note:** It is important to actually boil the jam mixture, not just heat it, as boiling kills any airborne spores that might be in the jam.

## VICTORIA SPONGE MIXTURE

| | 2-EGG MIXTURE | 3-EGG MIXTURE | 4-EGG MIXTURE | 5-EGG MIXTURE | 6-EGG MIXTURE | 8-EGG MIXTURE |
|---|---|---|---|---|---|---|
| softened butter or margarine | 115 g (4 oz) | 175 g (6 oz) | 225 g (8 oz) | 300 g (10 oz) | 350 g (12 oz) | 450 g (1 lb) |
| caster sugar | 115 g (4 oz) | 175 g (6 oz) | 225 g (8 oz) | 300 g (10 oz) | 350 g (12 oz) | 450 g (1 lb) |
| beaten eggs | 2 | 3 | 4 | 5 | 6 | 8 |
| self-raising flour | 115 g (4 oz) | 175 g (6 oz) | 225 g (8 oz) | 300 g (10 oz) | 350 g (12 oz) | 450 g (1 lb) |
| tablespoon hot water | 1 | 1 | 2 | 3 | 3 | 4 |
| | *Chocolate variation:* Blend 1 tablespoon cocoa powder with 1 tablespoon hot water, cool, then beat into mixture with butter and sugar. | *Chocolate variation:* Add same quantity of cocoa powder as for 2-egg mixture. | *Chocolate variation:* Blend 2 tablespoons cocoa powder with 2 tablespoons hot water, cool, then beat into mixture with butter and sugar. | *Chocolate variation:* Blend 3 tablespoons cocoa powder with 3 tablespoons hot water, cool, then beat into mixture with butter and sugar. | *Chocolate variation:* Add same quantity of cocoa powder as for 5-egg mixture. | *Chocolate variation:* Blend 4 tablespoons cocoa powder with 4 tablespoons hot water, cool, then beat into mixture with butter and sugar. |

# NUMBER CAKES

## QUICK MIX BIRTHDAY CAKE

115 g (4 oz) soft margarine
115 g (4 oz) caster sugar
2 large eggs
175 g (6 oz) self-raising flour
3 tablespoons evaporated milk
few drops vanilla essence

See each individual number cake recipe for tin size and timings. If using fan assisted ovens, follow manufacturer's instructions and reduce or alter the baking times and temperatures accordingly.

Grease and line tin. Preheat oven to 190C (375 F/Gas 4).

Place all the ingredients in a bowl and beat for 2 minutes with an electric beater or 3-4 minutes with a wooden spoon until smooth.

Spoon mixture into the tin and bake in the centre of the oven until light golden and firm to the touch. Leave in the tin for 4 minutes, then turn out to cool on a wire rack.

**Note:** The following number cakes are cooked in differently shaped tins, so use this recipe, which is designed to give evenly shaped cakes for cutting into numbers. The number one needs 575 g (1¼ lb) sugarpaste to cover it, the other numbers require about 900 g (2 lb).

### NUMBER ONE

Make a double quantity of basic recipe on page 12 and bake in two 25 × 7.5 cm (10 × 3 in) loaf tins for 40-45 minutes. Cool. Trim both cakes so that tops and ends are completely flat. Use one whole cake for the stem and cut the other one as shown for the base and top piece. Stick together on cake board with apricot glaze.

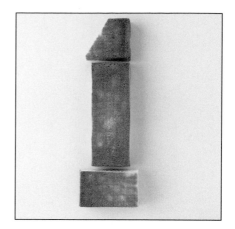

### NUMBER TWO

Make a triple quantity of basic recipe on page 12 and bake one third in a 25 × 7.5 cm (10 × 3 in) loaf tin for 40-45 minutes, and two thirds in a 29 × 18 × 5 cm (11 × 7 × 2 in) cake tin for 1 hour. Cut larger cake as shown for top and stem. Stick together on cake board with apricot glaze.

### NUMBER THREE

Make a double quantity of basic recipe on page 12 and bake in two 20 cm (8 in) ring tins for 35-40 minutes. Cut the cakes as shown and assemble using one ring for the top and the other for the base.

### NUMBER FOUR

Make a double quantity of basic recipe on page 12 and bake in a 28 × 18 × 5 cm (11 × 7 × 2 in) cake tin for 1 hour. Cut lengthways into 3 equal strips, 28 × 6 cm (11 × 2⅓ in) each. Cut pieces as shown and assemble on cake board. Stick together with apricot glaze.

## NUMBER FIVE

Make a double quantity of basic recipe on page 12 and bake half in a 20 cm (8 in) ring tin for 35-40 minutes and the other half in a 25 × 7.5 cm (10 × 3 in) loaf tin for 45 minutes. Cut out a quarter of the ring as shown, then assemble a piece of it with the cut straight pieces, securing with a wooden cocktail stick. Stick together with apricot glaze. Remove cocktail stick before serving.

## NUMBER SIX

Make a double quantity of basic recipe on page 12 and bake half in a 20 cm (8 in) ring tin for 35-40 minutes and the other half in a 25 × 7.5 cm (10 × 3 in) loaf tin for 45 minutes. Cut the straight cake and assemble with the ring cake as shown. Stick together with apricot glaze.

## NUMBER SEVEN

Make a double quantity of basic recipe on page 12 and bake in two 25 × 7.5 cm (10 × 3 in) loaf tins for 45 minutes. Cut cakes as shown, assemble and stick together with apricot glaze.

## NUMBER EIGHT

Make a double quantity of basic recipe on page 12 and bake in two 20 cm (8 in) ring tins for 35-45 minutes. Cut one cake as shown, then position both cakes on cake board and secure the join with apricot glaze.

## NUMBER NINE

Make a double quantity of basic recipe on page 12 and bake half in a 20 cm (8 in) ring tin for 35-45 minutes and the other half in a 15 × 7.5 cm (10 × 3 in) loaf tin for 45 minutes. Cut the straight cake as shown and assemble on cake board with the ring cake, securing with apricot glaze.

## NUMBER NOUGHT

Make one quantity of basic recipe on page 12 and bake in a 20 cm (8 in) ring tin for 35-45 minutes.

## NUMBERS 10-19

Use the above for numbers 2-9 but make a straight number one, using one quantity of basic recipe on page 12 baked in a 25 × 7.5 cm (10 × 3 in) loaf tin for 40-45 minutes.

This straight-sided number one gives you more room on the board to accommodate 2 numbers. An extra large cake board is needed for double numbers.

# COVERING CAKES

## COVERING WITH ALMOND PASTE

Brush sides of cake with apricot glaze. Sprinkle a surface with icing or caster sugar and knead almond paste until softened. Patch any gaps or holes in the cake with small scraps of almond paste. Roll out a strip long enough to go round sides of cake. Loosely roll up almond paste into a coil, then roll round sides of cake.

Roll out remaining almond paste to 0.5 cm (¼ in) thickness, the same shape as top of cake, plus an overlap of 1 cm (½ in). Lay almond paste on top of cake, pressing the overlap into the sides to give an even edge.

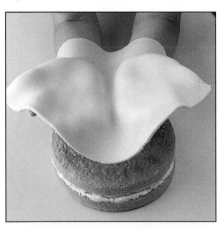

## COVERING WITH SUGARPASTE

Soften sugarpaste by kneading it well, then roll out on a surface dusted with icing sugar. Move the rolled sugarpaste to prevent it from sticking. Measure the circumference of the cake and roll out sugarpaste 2.5-5 cm (1-2 in) larger to cover whole cake. Lift sugarpaste carefully onto cake, holding it flat with both hands. Dust your hands with icing sugar and smooth into position, fluting out the bottom edges. Do not pleat the icing as this will leave a line.

Smooth down the sugarpaste in one direction to remove any air bubbles under the icing. Press the icing down firmly, then trim away the edges with a sharp knife. If any air bubbles remain under the cake, prick them with a pin and smooth over. Use the palm of your hand or a smoother to flatten and smooth over the top and sides.

# PIPING

## MAKING A PAPER PIPING BAG

Cut out a square of non-stick or silicone paper. This is stronger than ordinary greaseproof paper. Fold diagonally into 2 triangles. Curl the paper round into the centre.

Curl the paper into a cone and fold over the join to secure.

## BASIC PIPING

Snip a small hole at base of piping bag and insert the nozzle. Drop a tablespoon of butter cream or royal icing into the bag and fold over the top to seal in the icing.

Hold the bag so that the folded over section is secure, at a 45 degree angle and apply a little pressure. Push out the icing, pulling the bag away from the cake at the same time.

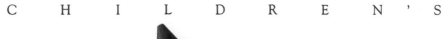

# CHEEKY CLOWN

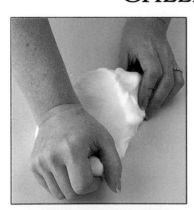

one quantity of 4-egg Victoria Sponge mixture, baked
in two 20 cm (8 in) sandwich tins at 180C
(350 F/Gas 4) for 30 minutes
30cm (12 in) square cake board
FOR THE DECORATION:
4 tablespoons apricot glaze (see page 10)
700 g (1½ lb) sugarpaste ready-to-roll icing
red, yellow and green paste food colourings
2 pink marshmallows and 2 orange jelly sweets
liquorice shoelaces
1 paper doily and 1 paper party hat
sugar-coated chocolate sweets

Knead 450 g (1 lb) sugarpaste icing to soften.

Place the cake centrally on the board and
brush with apricot glaze. Roll out sugarpaste
and cover cake. Trim edges, and keep white
scraps airtight. Colour 55 g (2 oz) sugarpaste
bright red. Roll 25 g (1 oz) into a ball for the
nose and roll out remainder thinly and cut
out a banana-shaped piece for the mouth.
Dampen with water and stick on cake.
Dampen and position 2 pink marshmallows
for cheeks.

Position 2 orange sweets for eyes, then cut strips of liquorice to outline eyes and make the crosses as picture. Press into sugarpaste icing. Make the mouth smile by pressing a piece of liquorice in a half-moon shape in the centre.

Colour 25 g (1 oz) sugarpaste green, and 85 g (3 oz) yellow. Roll out yellow sugarpaste and cut into long thin strips, then position in loops for the hair. Dampen and stick down.

Make the frill. Loosely pleat the paper doily and flute out the edges. Moisten a scrap of white sugarpaste with water, and use to stick the frilled doily under the clown's chin.

Roll the green sugarpaste out thickly and mould into a bow tie shape. Dampen and position on the frill. Decorate bow tie with sweets. Place paper party hat on clown's head.

*Serves 8-10.*

# MONSTER

one quantity of 3-egg Victoria Sponge mixture, baked
  in a 17.5 × 27.5 cm (7 × 11 in) cake tin at 160C
  (325F/Gas 3) for 40 minutes
35 cm (14 in) square cake board
FOR THE DECORATION:
225 g (8 oz) butter cream (see page 10)
2 white chocolate finger biscuits
350 g (12 oz) sugarpaste ready-to-roll icing
green food colouring
1 white marshmallow
selection of sweets for decoration
red and black liquorice

Trim the 2 top corners of the cake away as
shown to make a curved top.

Cover top and sides of cake with butter cream
and place on the cake board. Position biscuits
for arms. Colour the sugarpaste icing green,
and roll out to an oval shape with a straight
edge as shown. Drape over the cake and flute
up the bottom edge of the icing. Smooth
down the top and centre areas.

Cut the marshmallow in half and position for
eyes. Place a jelly sweet on each eye. Make a
mouth with liquorice and 2 sweets. Cut
strands of liquorice into short pieces for hair.
Decorate the monster with sweets as shown.

*Serves 8-10.*

# PIRATE

one quantity of 4-egg Victoria Sponge mixture, baked
   in two 20 cm (8 in) sandwich tins at 180C
   (350 F/ Gas 4) for 30 minutes
25 cm (10 in) round cake board
FOR THE DECORATION:
700 g (1½ lb) sugarpaste ready-to-roll icing
pink, blue and black paste food colourings
8 tablespoons apricot glaze (see page 10)
1 jelly peardrop sweet
2 marshmallows
1 blue liquorice allsort sweet
black bootlace liquorice
12 sugar-coated chocolate sweets
chocolate coins

Place cake on board. Colour 450 g (1 lb)
sugarpaste flesh pink. Spread cakes with
apricot glaze, sandwich together, then brush
over top and sides of cake. Roll out pink
sugarpaste and cover cake, then smooth and
trim. Reserve a scrap of white sugarpaste,
then colour remainder blue and a scrap black.
Stick on peardrop sweet for nose and position
marshmallows for cheeks. Colour a scrap of
sugarpaste red and roll out for a mouth. Roll
white into a round, stick on for eye and place
blue sweet on it. Roll out black scrap for eye
patch, dampen and stick in place.

Cut liquorice and position for eye patch
strap. Cut a short liquorice moustache and
position. Roll out blue sugarpaste icing
thinly. Lightly brush top of cake with water.
Drape the blue icing over top of cake to form
a scarf and pleat into folds. Screw up the ends
and flute one side to look like fabric.
Decorate with coloured sweets. Add gold
coins to cake and cake board.

*Serves 8-10.*

# TABBY CAT

one quantity of 4-egg Victoria Sponge mixture, baked in two 20 cm (8 in) sandwich tins at 180C (350F/ Gas 4) for 30 minutes
25 cm (10 in) square cake board
FOR THE DECORATION:
350 g (12 oz) butter cream or American soft icing (see page 10)
85 g (3 oz) long stranded desiccated coconut
115 g (4 oz) sugarpaste ready-to-roll icing
red bootlace liquorice
2 green jelly sweets
red paste food colouring
long strands of spaghetti

Sandwich cakes together with a little butter cream or American soft icing.

Cut out a wedge of cake at the top to make the shape for the ears, then place this wedge at the base for the bow tie. Place cake on a board. Stick bow tie piece in place with butter cream, then spread the butter cream all over top and sides of cake and flick up with a palette knife to represent the fur.

Toast one quarter of the coconut a light brown by placing on a sheet of foil and grilling for 2-3 minutes. Sprinkle the white coconut all over cake, then sprinkle the toasted coconut in three 'V'-shaped patterns on the top and sides of the cake.

Roll out 25 g (1 oz) sugarpaste white icing and cut 2 oval shapes for eyes. Position on cake. Outline the eyes with liquorice and press green sweets into the centre. Colour 25 g (1 oz) butter cream pink, spread in 2 triangles in the ears. Sprinkle with a few shreds of the coconut.

Colour 25 g (1 oz) sugarpaste red and shape into a nose and a tongue. Press nose onto cake, then make mouth outline with liquorice. Press tongue into mouth.

Colour remaining 55 g (2 oz) sugarpaste pink and make into a bow. Place on cake below chin. Press long strands of spaghetti into cake for whiskers.

*Serves 8-10.*

# RABBIT

one quantity of 4-egg Victoria Sponge mixture, baked
   in two 20 cm (8 in) sandwich tins at 180C
   (350F/Gas 4) for 30 minutes
30 × 35 cm (12 × 14 in) oblong cake board
FOR THE DECORATION:
450 g (1 lb) butter cream (see page 10)
pink, red, black, orange and green food colourings
115 g (4 oz) desiccated coconut
115 g (4 oz) sugarpaste ready-to-roll icing
2 white marshmallows and 2 pink sweets
red and black bootlace liquorice

Trim away 2 'V'-shapes from top of one cake.
Cut out ears and paw shapes from other cake
as shown and place in position.

Colour butter cream icing a light pink and
spread all over the shapes. Colour scraps of
butter cream a darker pink and spread inside
the ears. Sprinkle the coconut all over the
rabbit.

Divide sugarpaste icing and colour 55 g (2 oz) orange, 25 g (1 oz) green, 15 g (½ oz) red and leave 15 g (½ oz) white. Position marshmallows and pink sweets for eyes, then cut liquorice into strips and snip to make eyelashes. Position over eyes.

Make a nose from red sugarpaste and place in position. Make two long white teeth. Cut red liquorice to make mouth outline and black to make whiskers. Position teeth. Cut liquorice to make claws.

To make carrot, cut scrap of cake into a conical shape. Cover with butter cream. Roll out orange icing thinly and cover the cake. Mark on ridges with a fork.

To make leafy carrot top, roll out green icing thinly to an oblong. Cut two-thirds of the way down the sugarpaste icing as shown, then roll up loosely. Dampen the end with water and place on top of the orange carrot. Position it by the rabbit.

*Serves 10-12.*

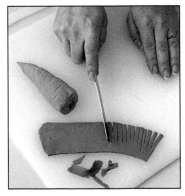

# BIRTHDAY BRICKS

one quantity of 5-egg Victoria Sponge mixture, baked
in a 20 cm (8 in) square tin at 180C (350F/Gas 4)
for 1¼ hours
35 cm (14 in) square cake board
FOR THE DECORATION:
10 tablespoons apricot glaze (see page 10)
1 kg (2¼ lb) sugarpaste ready-to-roll icing
yellow, pale blue and pink paste food colourings

Slice any bumps from top of cake so it is
completely flat. Cut cake into sixteen 5 cm
(2 in) squares.

Brush each square all over with apricot glaze
and keep on a wire rack. Divide sugarpaste
icing into quarters, leave one quarter white
and colour remaining quarters yellow, pale
blue and pink. (Alternatively, vary these
proportions, if wished.)

Roll out icing to 20 × 5 cm (8 × 2 in) strips. Place a square of cake in the centre of each one and roll the icing up over it to cover 4 sides.

Roll out remaining icing. Position covered cake cubes as shown, with the plain jam covered side on the sugarpaste. Cut round the square with a sharp knife. Repeat with the other plain side.

Smooth over and pinch the edges to make neat joins. Mould the brick in your hands to make the sides smooth. Crimp the edges, all round, using a crimper. Make 4 blue, 4 pink, 4 yellow and 4 white squares.

Roll out sugarpaste scraps and cut out shapes, animals and flowers. Dampen the back of each one with a little water and stick to the bricks as shown. Pile up into a pyramid.

*Serves 16.*

**Variations:** If you don't want to make the decorations by hand, use bought sugar letters or shapes from supermarkets.

For a colourful effect, make multi-coloured bricks, with a differently coloured square for each side.

# ──────ROCKING HORSE──────

one quantity of 4-egg Victoria Sponge mixture, baked
    in two 20 cm (8 in) round sandwich tins at 180C
    (350F/Gas 4) for 30 minutes
30 cm (12 in) square cake board
FOR THE DECORATION:
4 tablespoons apricot glaze (see page 10)
900 g (2 lb) sugarpaste ready-to-roll icing
red, black, yellow, orange and brown paste food
    colourings
silver balls
sugar birthday letters (optional)

Sandwich cakes together with apricot glaze.
Trim top of cake flat if it has peaked. Place on
cake board and brush all over with glaze.

Colour three quarters of the sugarpaste red,
roll out and drape over cake. Smooth down
over cake and trim away edges. Smooth top
so that it is completely flat. Divide remaining
sugarpaste and colour 55 g (2 oz) grey, 55 g
(2 oz) yellow, 25 g (1 oz) orange and 25 g
(1 oz) brown. Leave remainder white. Copy
the template of the pony opposite onto a
piece of cardboard. Roll out the grey sugarpaste, place the template on top and cut
round. Dampen the back of the sugarpaste
and stick onto the cake.

Push yellow sugarpaste through a garlic press
to make the mane and tail. Roll out orange
sugarpaste to make rockers, brown for bridle,
saddle (see template) and hooves and a
quarter of white for patterns on horse. Roll
out remaining white and red scraps into long
thin sausages, then twist the two together.
Dampen base of cake, then press on the strip.
Decorate the saddle and rockers with silver
balls. Stick on bought letters to say 'Happy
Birthday', if wished.

*Serves 8-12.*

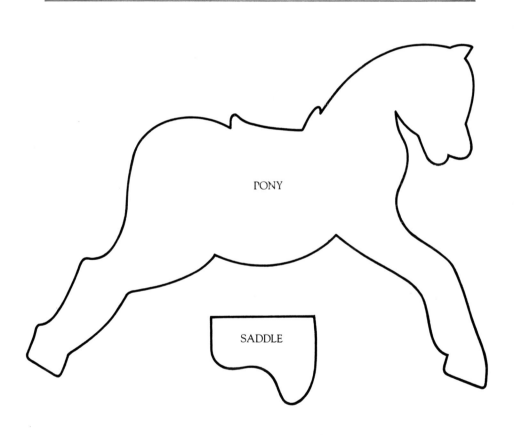

PONY

SADDLE

# CLOCK

one quantity of 4-egg Victoria Sponge mixture, baked
   in two 20 cm (8 in) round sandwich tins at 180C
   (350F/Gas 4) for 30 minutes
30 cm (12 in) square cake board
FOR THE DECORATION:
6 tablespoons apricot glaze (see page 10)
450 g (1 lb) sugarpaste ready-to-roll icing
yellow and red paste food colourings
black and red bootlace liquorice
coloured sweets

Sandwich 2 sponge cakes together with 2
tablespoons apricot glaze and place on board.
Trim top completely level if it has peaked.

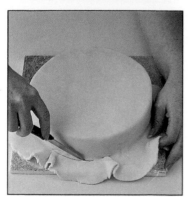

Leave 25 g (1 oz) sugarpaste icing white, then
colour remaining sugarpaste creamy yellow.
Brush cake with remaining apricot glaze,
then cover with yellow sugarpaste icing.
Smooth down and trim away edges, then roll
a rolling pin across the top to flatten completely. Trim away scraps of icing and colour
them red.

Make numbers 1-12 by rolling long thin sausages of red sugarpaste. Line them up in a row to check they are all the same height, then place on cake. Position 12 opposite 6, the 3 opposite 9, then fill in remaining numbers.

Make clock hands from black liquorice and place in the centre of cake with a small round of red sugarpaste and a sweet in the centre. Position the hands to the number corresponding to the age of the child.

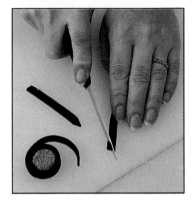

Mould the white sugarpaste into an oval shape for the body of the mouse, with a red liquorice tail. Place two red sweets on for eyes and one for nose, and mould 2 small pink ears. Place on cake.

Decorate the outside of cake with coloured sweets in 2 circles. Wrap two long strips of red liquorice round the outside edges and press into the sugarpaste.

*Serves 8-12.*

# TEDDY BEAR

one quantity of 5-egg Victoria Sponge mixture, divided
  between and baked in a 850 ml (30 floz/3¾ cup)
  pudding basin for 1½ hours, a 550 ml (20 floz/2½
  cup) pudding basin for 1¼ hours and a 20 cm (8 in)
  round sandwich tin at 160C (325F/Gas 3) for 30
  minutes
35 × 30 cm (14 × 12 in) oblong cake board
FOR THE DECORATION:
450 g (1 lb) butter cream (see page 10)
1 white marshmallow, 2 brown and 3 red sugar-coated
  chocolate sweets
175 g (6 oz) sugarpaste ready-to-roll icing
yellow, black, brown and red paste food colourings

Cut both pudding basin cakes so that tops are
completely flat.

Turn them over so that the domed sides are
upright. Cut a thin wedge from top of large
cake. Cut round cake into 2 ear pieces, 2 arms
and 2 legs as shown. Sculpt the small cake
into a dip for the eyes, then build up the snout
with scraps, sticking in place with butter
cream.

Trim grooves in legs to make feet. Position the pieces on the board as shown and stick them together with butter cream. Colour the remaining butter cream a yellowish brown for the teddy's fur.

Cut marshmallow in half for the eyes, then colour 25 g (1 oz) sugarpaste black, 55 g (2 oz) brown, 55 g (2 oz) red and a scrap pink. Shape paws, nose, mouth, ears and a red bow tie. Place brown sweets on eyes.

Completely cover the bear with butter cream, flicking up with a palette knife to make a furry effect.

Position eyes, nose, ears and mouth pieces on the face, press on the paws, then make claws from thinly rolled black sugarpaste. Place on the bow tie and red sweets as buttons.

*Serves 12.*

# —— PIERROT DOLL ——

one quantity of 4-egg Victoria Sponge mixture, divided between and baked in a 850 ml (30 fl oz / 3¾ cup) ovenproof pudding basin for 1½ hours, a 550 ml (20 fl oz / 2½ cup) pudding basin for 1¼ hours at 160C (325F/Gas 3)
35 × 30 cm (14 × 12 in) oblong cake board, or a tea tray covered in foil
4 bought mini swiss rolls
FOR THE DECORATION:
6 tablespoons apricot glaze (see page 10)
1.1 kg (2½ lb) sugarpaste ready-to-roll icing
black, flesh and red paste food colourings
pink powder food colouring

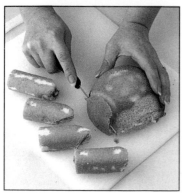

Trim tops of both cakes if they are peaked, so that they sit flat. Turn the cakes over. Trim the smaller one to an oval face shape as shown. Trim one end of the swiss rolls to make arms and legs as shown. Cover all the pieces with apricot glaze. Colour 700 g (1½ lb) sugarpaste grey, 225 g (8 oz) flesh colour and 115 g (4 oz) black. Roll out the flesh colour to an oval and cover the head. Smooth down and trim. Keep scraps airtight in a plastic bag.

Roll out grey sugarpaste and cover body, arms and legs. Keep grey scraps airtight. Position pieces as shown on cake board. Re-roll the remaining grey sugarpaste to an oblong large enough to cover the central body.

Position grey sugarpaste over body and flute up edges to represent a pierrot costume. Roll out black sugarpaste thinly and carve a half moon shaped piece for hat. Dampen top of head with water and stick on hat, smooth down and trim if necessary. Cover feet with scraps for shoes. Re-roll flesh-coloured sugarpaste scraps and stick onto arms, for hands.

Take remaining 115 g (4 oz) white sugarpaste and roll out thinly. Cut out a 7.5 cm (3 in) circle using a fluted cutter. Cut out a 4 cm (1½ in) plain disc from the centre of the circle. Take a wooden cocktail stick and roll it back and forwards over the edges until the icing flutes up. Cut out 5 layers of frills and stick round the neck. Roll out 2 more frills, halve and place 2 round wrists and 2 round ankles.

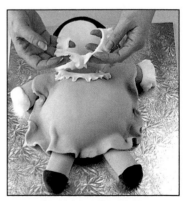

To make the face, cut out 4 tiny diamonds and 2 small circles from black sugarpaste. Colour a scrap of sugarpaste red, then cut out a mouth. Roll a scrap of flesh colour into a small ball for the nose. Position pieces as shown, then lightly mark on cheeks by dusting with a little pink food colouring powder. Make balls of red, white and black sugarpaste to decorate the front of the costume.

*Serves 12.*

# ———— JACK-IN-THE-BOX ————

one quantity of 5-egg Victoria Sponge mixture, divided
  between and baked in a 15 cm (6 in) square deep cake
  tin for 1 hour and a 550 ml (20 fl oz/2½ cup)
  greased ovenproof pudding basin for 40 minutes at
  160C (325F/Gas 3)
20 cm (8 in) square cake board
FOR THE DECORATION:
8 tablespoons apricot glaze (see page 10)
800 g (1¾ lb) sugarpaste ready-to-roll icing
yellow, red, blue and pink paste food colourings
85 g (3 oz) white almond paste
2 finger biscuits and 1 ice cream cone
black bootlace liquorice and coloured sweets

Trim any bumps from top of square cake to
make a completely flat surface.

Brush top and sides of cake with apricot glaze.
Place on cake board. Colour 350 g (12 oz)
sugarpaste icing yellow, roll out to a square
and drape over cake. Smooth down over the
cake and trim away edges.

Smooth the sides flat and pinch or crimp the sides to form straight edges. Colour 85 g (3 oz) sugarpaste red and roll into a long thin sausage. Roll out 85 g (3 oz) white sugarpaste in the same way, then twist the two together. Dampen top and base of sides of cake, then press on the twisted strips.

Colour 225 g (8 oz) sugarpaste blue. Trim pudding basin cake so that base is flat and brush with apricot glaze. Roll out blue icing, drape over and smooth down over cake. Place in centre of square cake.

Stick 2 finger biscuits into blue cake for arms. Roll out 25 g (1 oz) white sugarpaste and cut out a 7.5 cm (3 in) circle. Frill up the edges with a wooden cocktail stick (see page 35). Stick onto blue cake.

Make a ball of almond paste. Colour 25 g (1 oz) sugarpaste pink, dampen almond paste and drape pink icing over. Stick on pieces of liquorice for hair and sweets for face as shown. Roll out red sugarpaste scraps thinly, dab ice cream cone with apricot glaze and cover with red icing. Place on head. Decorate with sweets as shown.

*Serves 12-14.*

**Variation:** Make twisted strips for the sides of the cake as well, if wished.

# TOY BOX

one quantity of 5-egg Victoria Sponge mixture, baked
  in a 20 cm (8 in) square cake tin at 160C
  (325F/Gas 3) for 1¼ hours
25 cm (10 in) square cake board
FOR THE DECORATION:
115 g (4 oz) butter cream (see page 10)
1.25 kg (2¾ lb) sugarpaste ready-to-roll icing
yellow, red, brown, blue, green, yellow, black and
  orange paste food colourings

Cut a 5 cm (2 in) wide slice away from one
side of cake to make an oblong shape. Spread
cake with butter cream and place on board.

Colour 225 g (8 oz) sugarpaste yellow, 225 g
(8 oz) red, 175 g (6 oz) brown and 115 g (4 oz)
blue. Roll out the brown sugarpaste to cover
top, trim and smooth down. Roll out red and
yellow sugarpaste and cover the alternate
sides as shown. Roll out the blue sugarpaste
into a long sausage and press round top, side
and base joins.

Colour remaining sugarpaste various colours
and model toys of your choice such as a teddy,
football, doll, bricks, balls, car, chessboard,
palette. Cut out the letters 'Toys' and stick to
the side of the toy box, if wished.

*Serves 8.*

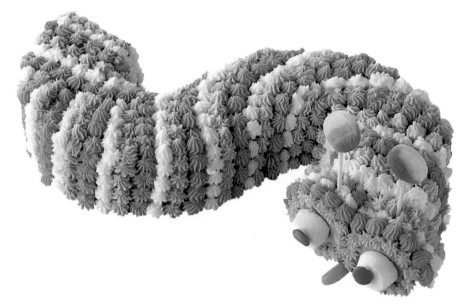

# CATERPILLAR

one quantity of 4-egg Victoria Sponge mixture, baked
in two 20 cm (8 in) round sandwich tins at 180C
(350F/Gas 4) for 30 minutes
35 × 30 cm (14 × 12 in) oblong cake board
FOR THE DECORATION:
450 g (1 lb) American soft icing (see page 10)
green and pink paste food colourings
2 marshmallows
2 round sweets and 1 long green sweet
2 lollipops

Place two cakes on top of each other. Cut a
5 cm (2 in) round from centre of cakes. Cut
remaining ring to form 2 half-moon shapes.
Remove sponge circles.

Sandwich half-moon shapes together with
a little American soft icing. Stick the 2 pieces
together on the board with a little icing to
form an 'S' shape. Divide icing into 3
portions, colour one green, one pink and
leave one white. Put into 3 piping bags fitted
with large star nozzles. Stick the two circles to
the front of cake to form eyes.

Pipe alternate lines of green, white and pink
across caterpillar's body. Stick marshmallows
to the eyes and press a round sweet into the
centre of each. Push a long green sweet into
the mouth and press 2 lollipops into tops of
eyes.

*Serves 12.*

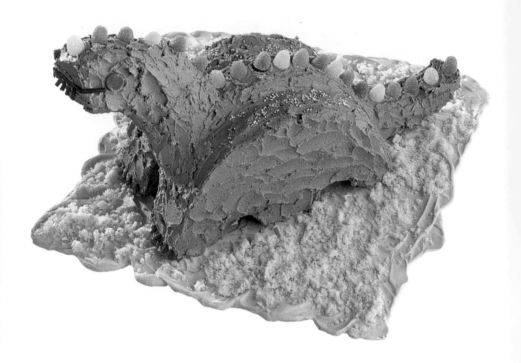

# DINOSAUR

one quantity of 4-egg Victoria Sponge mixture, baked
   in two 20 cm (8 in) round sandwich tins at 180C
   (350F/Gas 4) for 30 minutes
35 cm (14 in) square cake board
FOR THE DECORATION:
450 g (1 lb) butter cream (see page 10)
green and yellow paste food colourings
red bootlace liquorice for mouth and toes
jelly sweets
3 tablespoons granulated sugar

Cut one cake in half, sandwich together with
a little butter cream, then cut out 2 circles as
shown to form the feet.

Cut the other cake in pieces as shown,
following the diagram on page 118.

Colour three quarters of the butter cream green and one quarter yellow. Spread the yellow butter cream on the board. Separate the 2 sandwiched pieces and place the body piece between them. Place the tailpiece in position, securing it with a little butter cream.

Position the neck piece, securing it with 2 wooden cocktail sticks.

Spread the green butter cream all over the dinosaur with a palette knife. Cut out strips of liquorice for teeth and mouth and to mark the toes and press them into the butter cream.

Place jelly sweets all down the back to form spines. Colour the granulated sugar. Place in a bowl, add a spot of yellow paste colouring and stir well. Sprinkle the sugar round the dinosaur to make sand. When slicing cake, make sure wooden cocktail sticks are removed.

*Serves 12.*

## LION

one quantity of 4-egg Victoria Sponge mixture, baked
   in two 20 cm (8 in) round sandwich tins at 180C
   (350F/Gas 4) for 30 minutes
30 cm (12 in) round cake board
FOR THE DECORATION:
450 g (1 lb) butter cream (see page 10)
55 g (2 oz) white almond paste
1 mini swiss roll
yellow, orange, red and black paste food colourings
115 g (4 oz) sugarpaste ready-to-roll icing
red bootlace liquorice
2 green jelly sweets

Sandwich cakes together with butter cream.
Cut top edges away in a curve as shown.

Stick cut pieces to the base edges with butter
cream. Place on cake board. Trim edges as
shown. Mould almond paste over the end of
the mini swiss roll. Trim into a long, raised
triangular shape for the nose and stick to
centre of cake with a little butter cream.

Colour two thirds of remaining butter cream pale orange and spread three quarters over cake, smoothing it flat over face and nose with a palette knife.

Put white butter cream in a piping bag with a large star nozzle and pipe on the mane and hair.

Colour remaining orange butter cream a bright, dark orange and place in piping bag. Outline and highlight whiskers and mane.

Roll out 25 g (1 oz) white sugarpaste into 2 ovals for eyes. Place in position and outline with red liquorice. Cut a slice off green jelly sweets and place sweets on eyes. Colour 50 g (2 oz) sugarpaste red and mould into a tongue. Press into place. Colour 25 g (1 oz) black, mould into a nose and press on.

*Serves 8.*

# BROWN OWL

one quantity of 6-egg Victoria Sponge mixture, baked
   in a 30 × 20 cm (12 × 8 in) oblong tin at 160C
   (325F/Gas 3) for 1¼ hours
35 × 30 cm (14 × 12 in) oblong cake board
FOR THE DECORATION:
175 g (6 oz) chocolate butter cream (see page 10)
1.25 kg (2¾ lb) sugarpaste ready-to-roll icing
brown, cream, yellow, black and white paste food
   colourings
edible yellow blusher

Cut the top edges of cake, and carve body
into a rounded shape as shown. Spread all
over with butter cream and place on cake
board.

Colour 575 g (1¼ lb) sugarpaste dark brown,
450 g (1 lb) beige, 115 g (4 oz) cream, 55 g
(2 oz) yellow, 25 g (1 oz) black and leave 25 g
(1 oz) white. Roll out half the beige sugarpaste and drape it over the body. Roll out
450 g (1 lb) dark brown sugarpaste thinly,
drape over head, trim, smooth down and
mould into the ears. Re-roll scraps and keep
airtight in a plastic bag.

Roll out two cream ovals and place on the face. Roll out 2 white discs and position on the ovals, then roll out 2 smaller black rounds and place on white discs. Place white dots in centre.

Roll out remaining beige sugarpaste and cut into 'V' shapes. Starting at the base, press on rows of 'V's overlapping as in the picture and ending underneath the face. Reserve the scraps.

Roll 2 long brown strips to go down each side of the body. Dampen and press on, slightly overlapping the feathers. Using the thick end of an icing nozzle, press feather patterns into the brown icing. To make feathers for face, roll out brown scraps, use a small star to cut these out, then halve stars.

Dampen stars and stick in position. Mould yellow sugarpaste into a beak and 6 claws. Moisten and stick in place as shown. Make 2 small triangles from beige sugarpaste scraps and position in ears, then mark pattern with a fork. Dab round eyes with yellow blusher.

*Serves 12.*

# ———— FROGS IN A LILY POND ————

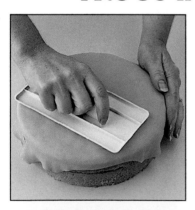

one quantity of 4-egg Victoria Sponge mixture, baked
   in two 20 cm (8 in) round sandwich tins at 180C
   (350F/Gas 4) for 30 minutes
30 cm (12 in) round cake board
FOR THE DECORATION:
8 tablespoons apricot glaze (see page 10)
575 g (1¼ lb) sugarpaste ready-to-roll icing
blue, green, yellow, orange, black and red paste food
   colourings

Sandwich cakes together and spread apricot
glaze over top and sides of cake. Colour 225 g
(8 oz) sugarpaste light blue and roll into a
circle to cover top and edges. Smooth down
top of cake.

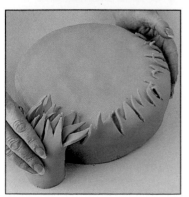

Colour 115 g (4 oz) green and roll into a strip
long enough to go round the sides of cake.
Cut a jagged edge with scissors to represent
rushes, then carefully wind up the strip and
unwind it round sides of cake.

Re-roll green scraps and cut out circles to form lily pads. Pinch and place on blue water. To make 6 white lilies, roll out 55 g (2 oz) white sugarpaste, cut out 6 rounds and snip edges with scissors. Colour scraps yellow and mould into small balls for lily centres.

Colour 115 g (4 oz) sugarpaste orange. Mould into heads and tails of goldfish (the bodies will be under the water). Make circles of white sugarpaste for eyes and yellow for mouths. Mark fish with end of a piping nozzle as shown.

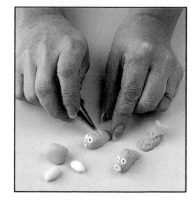

Colour 115 g (4 oz) sugarpaste green and model 2 frogs' bodies and cut mouths as shown. Make eyes from white sugarpaste and scraps coloured black.

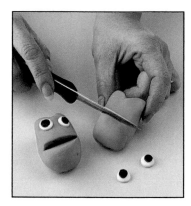

To make frogs' legs, roll a long strip of green sugarpaste, bend, stick to bodies and snip feet. Colour scraps of sugarpaste red and make a tongue for each frog.

*Serves 8-10.*

# ─── PONY IN A STABLE ───

one quantity of 4-egg Victoria Sponge mixture, baked
  in a 900 g (2 lb) loaf tin at 160C (325F/Gas 3) for
  1 ¼ hours
20 cm (8 in) square cake board
FOR THE DECORATION:
700 g (1 ½ lb) sugarpaste ready-to-roll icing
green, brown, black, yellow, red and blue paste food
  colourings
225 g (8 oz) butter cream (see page 10)
edible food pens in black and brown
red bootlace liquorice

Trim top of cake completely level and cut out
a cavity with an oval top and straight base as
shown.

Trim top and base ends so cake stands up
straight. Colour 115 g (4 oz) sugarpaste icing
green, roll out thinly, dab board with butter
cream and cover the board with sugarpaste.
Mark on grass with the tines of a fork.

Colour 450 g (1 lb) sugarpaste light brown, marbling it to give a wood effect. Cover cake with butter cream. Roll out brown sugarpaste to an oblong large enough to cover top and sides and drape over cake as shown. Smooth down, trim and re-roll trimmings. Cover back piece of stable. Mark on wooden slatted effect with a ruler.

Colour 25 g (1 oz) sugarpaste dark brown. Roll out thinly, then press into hollow section and round top of stable. Roll out light brown scraps into thin strips for planks. Dampen and stick to stable door and mark nails with an edible food pen. Stand stable upright on cake board.

Colour 50 g (2 oz) sugarpaste grey and mould into a pony's neck and head, making the base wide for support. Mould on nostrils and mouth. Place on a wooden cocktail stick and attach to stable. Support with an egg box until set.

Attach red liquorice harness. Make mane by pressing a scrap of yellow sugarpaste through a garlic press. Draw on the pony's eyes. To make a rosette, colour some scraps of sugarpaste red and blue. Roll out the red, blue and some white sugarpaste and stamp out 4 different sized rounds with icing nozzles. Flute edges of larger ones with a wooden cocktail stick then stick them together. Make thin strips for ribbons, then press rosette onto stable.

*Serves 8.*

# LADYBIRD

one quantity of 4-egg Victoria Sponge mixture, baked
   in a greased 3.3 litre (6 pint/ 14 cup) pudding basin,
   25 cm (10 in) wide at the top, at 160C (325F/Gas 3)
   for 1½ hours
30 cm (12 in) round cake board
FOR THE DECORATION:
6 tablespoons apricot glaze (see page 10)
620 g (1 lb 6 oz) sugarpaste ready-to-roll icing
red, black, brown and green paste food colourings
2 orange and 1 red sugar-coated chocolate sweets
115 g (4 oz) American soft icing (see page 10)
sugar flowers

Turn cake upside down. Trim away front of
cake to make a sloping nose shape.

Brush cake all over with apricot glaze. Colour
450 g (1 lb) sugarpaste red and 115 g (4 oz)
black and 55 g (2 oz) brown. Roll out the red
sugarpaste thinly, then drape over the cake.
Smooth down and tuck the edges under cake.
Roll out the black sugarpaste thinly to a
triangular shape, then dampen the front of
cake and drape the black sugarpaste over.
Press down, trim and crimp front edge.

Roll scraps of black sugarpaste into a thin
sausage and stick it down the middle of the
back to make a division for the wings. Stick
on sweets for the eyes and mouth. Roll the
brown icing into small balls, flatten each
ball, dampen then stick onto the red wings.
Colour American icing green, spread on the
board, then decorate with sugar flowers.

*Serves 8.*

# BUTTERFLY

one quantity of 4-egg Victoria Sponge mixture, baked
    in two 20 cm (8 in) round sandwich tins at 180C
    (350F/Gas 4) for 30 minutes
35 cm (14 in) square cake board
FOR THE DECORATION:
115 g (4 oz) butter cream (see page 10)
4 tablespoons apricot glaze (see page 10)
575 g (1¼ lb) sugarpaste ready-to-roll icing
lilac and pink paste food colourings
115 g (4 oz) royal icing (see page 10)
silver balls and candles

Sandwich cakes together with butter cream.
Cut in half and position halves on cake board
with rounded sides pointing inwards.

Brush cake with apricot glaze. Colour 350 g
(12 oz) sugarpaste lilac, roll out and drape
over each cake half and press into the curved
centre. Trim away edges and smooth down to
flatten top. Using crimpers, crimp all round
top edge.

Colour remaining sugarpaste pink. Make a
sausage shape from lilac scraps for the body.
Using small cutters, stamp out rounds, halve
and place in an overlapping pattern on the
body as shown. Decorate wings with royal
icing, silver balls and sugarpaste shapes
as shown. Place the candles in position as
shown.

*Serves 12.*

# HEDGEHOG

one quantity of 3-egg Victoria Sponge mixture, baked
   in a 1 litre (35 fl oz/4½ cup) pudding basin at 160C
   (325F/Gas 3) for 1¼ hours
30 cm (12 in) round cake board
FOR THE DECORATION:
4 tablespoons apricot glaze (see page 10)
115 g (4 oz) butter cream (see page 10)
55 g (2 oz) desiccated coconut
green, brown and black paste food colourings
450 g (1 lb) chocolate-flavoured sugarpaste ready-
   to-roll icing
25 g (1 oz) white sugarpaste ready-to-roll icing
115 g (4 oz) chocolate mint sticks

Turn cake upside down. Trim away front of
cake to make a sloping nose shape.

Brush all over with apricot glaze. Colour the
butter cream and coconut light green. Spread
green butter cream on the board, then press
on coconut. Roll out the chocolate sugarpaste to a circle large enough to cover the
body, drape over, trim and smooth. Mould
2 feet from trimmings, mark on claws and
position next to body.

Colour scraps black and mould into a nose
and 2 circles for eyes. Roll out white sugarpaste into 2 larger circles, stick on black
circles for pupils. Add the nose. Halve the
chocolate sticks and press into the body.

*Serves 8.*

# SNAIL

one quantity of 3-egg Chocolate Victoria Sponge
    mixture, baked in a 1 litre (35 fl oz/4½ cup) pudding
    basin at 160C (325F/Gas 3) for 1½ hours
2 bought mini chocolate swiss rolls
35 cm (12 in) square cake board
FOR THE DECORATION:
115 g (4 oz) butter cream (see page 10)
750 g (1 lb 10 oz) sugarpaste ready-to-roll icing
lilac, yellow, orange, pink, brown and green paste food
    colourings
sweets to decorate
115 g (4 oz) royal icing (see page 10)

Trim top of round cake flat and turn upside
down. Cut front from each swiss roll into a
slope as shown.

Spread all the pieces with butter cream.
Colour 225 g (8 oz) sugarpaste lilac, 300 g (10
oz) yellow and 55 g (2 oz) each of orange,
pink, blue, brown. Roll out the lilac sugarpaste and cover the 2 swiss rolls (snail's
body), moulding 2 horns on one and a curly
tail on the other. Roll out 225 g (8 oz) yellow
sugarpaste thinly and drape over round cake
(snail's shell). Trim and smooth down. Press
shell onto body on cake board.

Roll the different coloured sugarpastes into
long thin sausages, then wind them round the
shell in alternate colours, ending in the
centre with a spiral shape. Make a face with
the sweets. Press 2 cocktail sticks into the
head for horns, then place two small sugarpaste balls on the cocktail sticks. Colour
royal icing green and swirl onto cake board
with a palette knife.

*Serves 8.*

# PANDA

one quantity of 4-egg Chocolate Victoria Sponge
   mixture, baked in two 20 cm (8 in) round sandwich
   tins at 180C (350F/Gas 4) for 30 minutes
35 × 30 cm (14 × 12 in) oblong cake board
FOR THE DECORATION:
350 g (12 oz) American soft icing (see page 10)
225 g (8 oz) plain (dark) chocolate, grated
115 g (4 oz) desiccated coconut
150 g (5 oz) sugarpaste ready-to-roll icing
brown, black and orange paste food colourings
1 white marshmallow, 1 red sweet and 3 coloured
   sweets

Cut a 10 cm (4 in) round from side of one
cake, then cut away a small oval from the
round. Cut remaining shape into 6 pieces.

Place the uncut sponge on the board and
position the cut pieces as shown, trimming 2
of the crescent shapes for ears. Stick pieces
together with a little American icing. Colour
half of remaining icing black and leave
remainder white. Spread the white icing over
head, tummy and paws. Spread black icing
over sides of face, ears and body. Sprinkle
grated chocolate over black parts, and
coconut over the white parts.

To make the face, colour 25 g (1 oz) sugarpaste brown, 25 g (1 oz) black and 75 g (3 oz)
orange. Cut and layer the brown, white and
black shapes for eyes as shown. Position
marshmallow for nose. Position a red sweet
for tongue then 3 sweets as buttons. Make an
orange bow from sugarpaste and crimp edges.

*Serves 12.*

# CAR

one quantity of 4-egg Victoria Sponge mixture, baked
   in a 20 cm (8 in) round deep cake tin at 180C
   (350F/Gas 4) for 40 minutes
20 cm (8 in) round cake board
FOR THE DECORATION:
6 tablespoons apricot glaze (see page 10)
900 g (2 lb) sugarpaste ready-to-roll icing
yellow and black paste food colourings
red and black bootlace liquorice

Freeze the cake for 20 minutes to make cutting easier, then carve into the shape as
shown on page 118.

Build up bonnet with extra trimmings, stick
on with a little apricot glaze and trim flat.
Coat the cake all over with glaze. Colour
700 g (1½ lb) sugarpaste yellow, 115 g (4 oz)
black and leave 115 g (4 oz) white. Roll out
yellow sugarpaste, drape over cake, smooth
down and trim. Roll out black sugarpaste and
stamp out four 4 cm (1½ in) thick rounds for
wheels. Moisten and stick to base.

Roll out yellow sugarpaste scraps and stamp
out 4 smaller circles for centre of wheels.
Stick in position. Make 2 small black rounds
for headlamps. Roll out white sugarpaste and
cut out 6 windows, 2 centres for headlamps
and a number plate. Outline doors, windows
and bonnet with red liquorice. Cut 2 small
strips of black liquorice for windscreen wipers
and 4 red for door handles. With the tip of a
knife, outline the radiator and petrol tank.

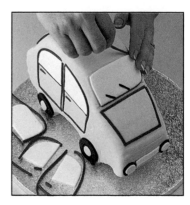

*Serves 8.*

# TRAIN

one quantity of 5-egg Victoria Sponge mixture, baked
in a 20 cm (8 in) square tin at 160C (325F/Gas 3)
for 1¼ hours
1 bought swiss roll
large oblong cake board or tea tray covered with foil
FOR THE DECORATION:
12 tablespoons apricot glaze (see page 10)
575 g (1¼ lb) black sugarpaste ready-to-roll icing
1 kg (2¼ lb) green sugarpaste ready-to-roll icing
(see note)
575 g (1¼ lb) red sugarpaste ready-to-roll icing
115 g (4 oz) white sugarpaste ready-to-roll icing
115 g (4 oz) royal icing (see page 10)
orange paste food colouring
rice cereal
chocolate matchstick sweets and liquorice sweets

Cut cake into pieces as shown, slicing some
pieces into layers for base pieces. Slice swiss
roll in half and place on base pieces. Hollow
out centre of one oblong for the coal truck.

Coat all the pieces with apricot glaze. Roll out black sugarpaste and cover base pieces. Smooth over and trim. Model a funnel from a scrap of cake and cover with black sugarpaste. Roll out green sugarpaste and cover swiss roll pieces and top of coal truck. Smooth down and trim neatly.

Moisten black pieces lightly with water and press on to green pieces as shown. Roll out red sugarpaste and cover engine cab. Stamp out 4 small, 4 medium and 4 large wheels in thickly rolled red sugarpaste. Stick on funnel.

Trim carriages with strips of red sugarpaste and engine front as shown. Make 2 round red headlamps and trim with white circles. Roll out black scraps and stamp out circles to make wheel trims, and trim engine with a narrow strip of green, then stick on wheels and head-lamps. Roll out white sugarpaste and make 6 windows and 2 round porthole windows. Stick on and trim with thinly rolled strips of coloured sugarpaste.

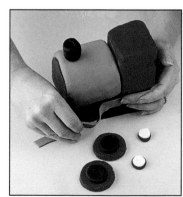

Colour the royal icing orange and spread onto board for the track. Sprinkle over the rice cereal, then press on chocolate matchsticks to make the rails. Carefully place engine, coal truck and carriage on track. Fill coal truck with liquorice logs.

*Serves 12.*

**Note:** It is easier to buy ready coloured sugar-paste for this cake, as it uses large amounts, and these will require a lot of paste food colouring.

# ───── AEROPLANE ─────

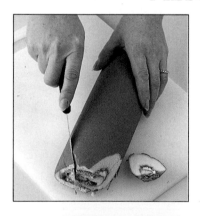

1 large bought swiss roll
oblong ice cream wafers
30 cm (12 in) square cake board
FOR THE DECORATION:
6 tablespoons apricot glaze (see page 10)
800 g (1¾ lb) sugarpaste ready-to-roll icing
black and blue paste food colourings
1 stick of rock
115 g (4 oz) royal icing (see page 10)
small red and yellow jelly sweets

Press swiss roll to flatten slightly, then trim front to a pointed cone all round. Keep trimmings. Brush all over with apricot glaze.

Colour 450 g (1 lb) sugarpaste grey, 85 g (3 oz) black and 225 g (8 oz) blue. Leave remainder white. Keep sugarpaste wrapped in airtight polythene bags. Cut wafers as shown on page 118 and sandwich together with larger piece on bottom and other 2 pieces placed on top, with narrowest piece as wing tip. For tailpiece, cut one wafer in half diagonally and cut 2 smaller pieces. Cover thinly with royal icing. Roll out blue sugarpaste and cover wafers. Place blue wing and tail pieces flat on plastic wrap and leave to harden for 2-3 hours.

Roll out grey sugarpaste and completely cover body of plane. Smooth down over swiss roll, tuck underneath and trim away. Completely smooth to a torpedo shape with your palms. Mould 2 blue rounds for engine exhausts for back of plane.

Cut rock into two 4 cm (1½ in) strips and one 6 cm (2½ in) strip for the wheels. Roll out grey icing and cover wheels. Squash a piece of swiss roll trimming, form into a pad and cover with grey sugarpaste. Cut out front windscreen and side windows from white sugarpaste. Moisten with water and stick onto plane.

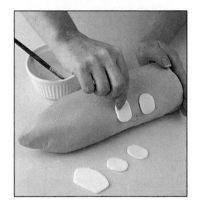

Roll out black sugarpaste and cover wheel ends. Roll out black trimmings to a long thin sausage and trim windows and windscreen. Make a door. Position wheels and pad under plane.

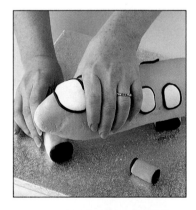

Carefully stick the hardened blue wings onto wheels with royal icing (support with screwed up plastic wrap until ready to serve). Position tail pieces and stick together with royal icing. Trim tailpiece with black strip as shown. Stick red and yellow jelly sweets onto back of plane and wings for lights.

*Serves* 8.

## ——————— MAN IN THE MOON ———————

one quantity of 4-egg Victoria Sponge mixture, baked
    in two 20 cm (8 in) round sandwich tins at 180C
    (350F/Gas 4) for 30 minutes
30 cm (12 in) round cake board
FOR THE DECORATION:
700 g (1½ lb) sugarpaste ready-to-roll icing
blue and yellow paste food colourings
4 tablespoons apricot glaze (see page 10)
silver balls

Colour 450 g (1 lb) sugarpaste dark blue and
225 g (8 oz) cream.

Brush cake with apricot glaze, roll out blue
sugarpaste, cover cake and trim. Smooth
completely flat and place on cake board.

Roll out cream sugarpaste thickly. Cut into a circle, then cut and mould into a half moon shape.

Dampen half the blue icing and stick the moon onto the cake. Mould eyes, nose and mouth.

Roll out cream sugarpaste scraps and cut out stars of different sizes using star cutters. Dampen stars and stick to cake.

Decorate background with silver balls. Place one silver ball on eye.

*Serves 8-10.*

# SPACESHIP

one quantity of 6-egg Victoria Sponge mixture, baked
    in three 20 cm (8 in) round sandwich tins at 180C
    (350F/Gas 4) for 30 minutes
30 cm (12 in) round cake board
FOR THE DECORATION:
115 g (4 oz) butter cream (see page 10)
1.1 kg (2½ lb) sugarpaste ready-to-roll icing
red bootlace liquorice and 8 black and white liquorice
    allsort sweets, small jelly sweets and 4 lollipops,
    silver balls and tiny coloured sugar balls
4 tablespoons royal icing (see page 10)
blue paste food colouring

Coat one cake with butter cream. Roll out
350 g (12 oz) white sugarpaste; cover cake.
Decorate with liquorice and silver balls.

Sandwich 2 remaining cakes together with
butter cream and press together firmly. Trim
away sides to form a disc shape.

Colour 700 g (1½ lb) sugarpaste blue. Coat cake with butter cream and roll out sugarpaste to completely cover cake. Smooth flat with the palms of your hands.

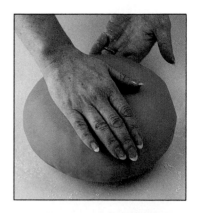

Spread top of white cake with royal icing. Sprinkle over coloured sugar balls, then press in 8 liquorice sweets to form the launch pad.

Roll out 115 g (4 oz) white sugarpaste to long strips for the windows. Cut into 8 windows, dampen and stick to top of ship. Outline windows with strips of dampened red liquorice.

Place ship on launch pad. Dab brightly coloured jelly sweets with royal icing and stick round sides of ship. Stick lollipops in centre of ship for sonic antennae.

*Serves 12.*

# ROCKET

1 large bought swiss roll
fan-shaped wafers
4 mini swiss rolls
ice cream cornet
35 cm (14 in) square cake board
FOR THE DECORATION:
115 g (4 oz) butter cream (see page 10)
115 g (4 oz) royal icing (see page 10)
1 kg (2¼ lb) sugarpaste ready-to-roll icing
yellow, red and blue paste food colourings
silver balls
12 small jelly sweets and pink liquorice sweets
small candles and holders

Pat large swiss roll to a round shape. Trim one
end to a point; spread with butter cream.

Stick ice cream cone to point of swiss roll and
cover with royal icing. (Don't use butter
cream as this makes the wafer go soggy).
Colour 800 g (1¾ lb) sugarpaste yellow, roll
out to an oblong and cover cake. Trim and
smooth down. Roll out trimmings.

Coat each of the mini swiss rolls with butter cream, then cover with yellow sugarpaste. Colour 115 g (4 oz) sugarpaste red and roll out. Make the fins. Spread fan wafers with royal icing, then cover with red sugarpaste. Leave to dry flat on plastic wrap for 3 hours to harden.

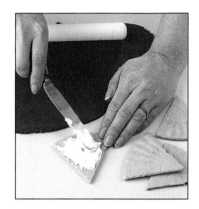

Cover cake trimmings with butter cream and yellow sugarpaste trimmings to make a slope. Stick to cake board, then position rocket on slope so it forms an angle.

Stick covered rolls to cake, securing with cocktail sticks. (Don't forget to remove these when serving the cake.)

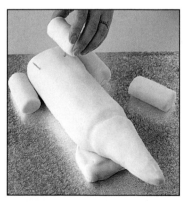

Colour 25 g (1 oz) sugarpaste red, 55 g (2 oz) blue and leave 25 g (1 oz) white. Roll blue icing into thin sausage, dampen and stick to nose cone and jets to outline. Stamp out stars from red, white and blue icing and decorate rocket. Stick silver balls in centre. Dab red fins with royal icing and stick in between rocket jets. Decorate body and jets with sweets. Position candles and holders in base, pointing upwards and away from the board.

*Serves 8-10.*

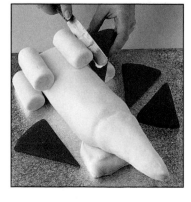

# ROBOT

one quantity of 5-egg Victoria Sponge mixture, baked
  in a 20 cm (8 in) square deep cake tin at 160C
  (325F/Gas 3) for 1¼ hours
25 cm (10 in) round cake board
FOR THE DECORATION:
900 kg (2 lb) sugarpaste ready-to-roll icing
yellow and purple paste food colourings
6 tablespoons apricot glaze (see page 10)
115 g (4 oz) royal icing (see page 10)
liquorice allsorts
red bootlace liquorice

Cut the cake as shown.

Cut 2 legs 10 × 4 cm (4 × 1½ in), 2 arms
8 × 4 cm (3½ × 1½ in), round head 7.5 cm
(3 in), body 8 × 7.5 cm (3½ × 3 in) and two
feet 1 × 5 cm (½ × 2 in). Carve head and
body into curved shapes. Trim pieces flat.

Colour 450 g (1 lb) sugarpaste yellow and 450 g (1 lb) sugarpaste purple. Roll out sugarpaste. Brush all cake pieces with apricot glaze.

Cover head, body and feet with yellow and arms and legs with purple sugarpaste. Smooth over joins to neaten.

Dab body pieces with royal icing and stick together. Leave to dry and set for 1-2 hours: support the arms with tall tins covered in plastic wrap.

Decorate body and face with square and round liquorice allsorts. Wind red bootlace liquorice round neck and waist.

*Serves 8-10.*

# SCOTTIE DOG

one quantity of 4-egg Victoria Sponge mixture, divided
between and baked in an 850 ml (30 fl oz/
3¾ cup) pudding basin for 1½ hours and a 550 ml
(20 floz/2½ cup) pudding basin for 1¼ hours at
160C (325F/Gas 3)
25 cm (10 in) round cake board
FOR THE DECORATION:
700 g (1½ lb) American soft icing (see page 10)
175 g (6 oz) sugarpaste ready-to-roll icing
black, brown, red and cream paste food colourings
tartan ribbon

Cut top of larger cake flat. Turn upside down
and place on cake board.

Turn small cake on its side. Cut away a piece
to make two ears and carve a nose shape, then
hollow out eyes and trim round face. Reserve
all the trimmings.

Stand smaller cake upright and stick onto front of larger cake with wooden cocktail sticks. (Remember to remove these when serving.)

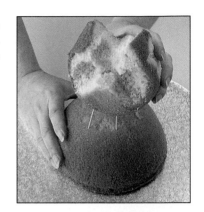

Make up gap at back of head with cut pieces of cake, sticking them on with American icing. Position 2 scraps for legs and another for the tail. Colour 85 g (3 oz) sugarpaste black, 25 g (1 oz) brown and 25 g (1 oz) red.

Roll out brown, white and black sugarpaste discs to make eyes. Make a white triangular flash for each eye. Spread a little icing onto face and fix eyes. Mould remaining black icing into a triangle and mark as a nose. Press onto face. Make a tongue with red sugarpaste and fix in place.

Place remaining American icing in a piping bag fitted with a star nozzle. Pipe icing all over dog. Flick with a fork to represent the coat. Paint a few flecks of brown and cream colouring onto coat. Make a tartan bow from ribbon and press into the icing.

*Serves 8-10.*

# FISH TANK

one quantity of 5-egg Victoria Sponge mixture, baked
   in a 20 cm (8 in) square tin at 160C (325F/Gas 3)
   for 1¼ hours
35 cm (14 in) square cake board
FOR THE DECORATION:
6 tablespoons apricot glaze (see page 10)
1.1 kg (2½ lb) sugarpaste ready-to-roll icing
blue, green, brown, yellow, orange and black paste
   food colourings

Trim top of cake completely flat. Cut
cake into 2 oblongs, spread one with apricot
glaze, then sandwich together on top of one
another.

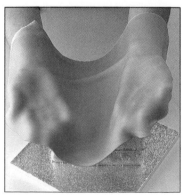

Colour the sugarpaste as follows: 700 g
(1½ lb) mottled blue, 85 g (3 oz) pale green,
45 g (1½ oz) dark green, 15 g (½ oz) brown,
25 g (1 oz) yellow, 15 g (½ oz) orange, 15 g
(½ oz) marbled black and white, 250 g (9 oz)
black. Brush cake all over with glaze then roll
out blue sugarpaste and cover cake; smooth
down and trim away edges.

Mould two large fish from yellow sugarpaste. Stick onto blue sugarpaste. Roll out orange sugarpaste and make 3 small orange fish. Mark on eyes and fins with a sharp knife.

Roll out light green sugarpaste and cut out long green leaves. Stick onto blue sugarpaste. Roll out dark green sugarpaste and cut out short green leaves, then intersperse them between the light green ones.

Cut out an anchor from brown sugarpaste and stick in one corner at an angle. Roll the marbled black and white sugarpaste into small stones and stick to the bottom of the tank.

Roll black sugarpaste into long thin strips 1 cm (½ in) wide. Dampen and stick round the top, sides and base of the tank.

*Serves 8.*

# ——RABBIT IN A HUTCH——

one quantity of 5-egg Victoria Sponge mixture, baked
   in a 20 cm (8 in) square, deep cake tin at 160C
   (325F/Gas 3) for 1¼ hours, then cooled and frozen
   until fairly solid
30 cm (12 in) square cake board
FOR THE DECORATION:
8 tablespoons apricot glaze (see page 10)
1 kg (2¼ lb) sugarpaste ready-to-roll icing
brown, pink, green, orange and yellow paste food
   colourings and brown food colouring pen
1 white marshmallow
strands thin spaghetti

Cut off a 4 cm (1½ in) strip, then place cut
strip down one end to make an oblong.

Trim top level. Stick cut strip to cake with
apricot glaze. Transfer rabbit pattern, (page
118) onto graph paper, cut out, then mark
onto cake, using a sharp knife. Carve round
pattern to a depth of 0.5 cm (¼ in), then
shave away cake to make a raised rabbit
shape.

Colour 575 g (1¼ lb) sugarpaste a marbled brown, by half kneading the colour in. Colour 115 g (4 oz) dark brown, 175 g (6 oz) pink, 55 g (2 oz) green, 55 g (2 oz) orange, 25 g (1 oz) yellow. Roll out dark brown icing. Brush background with apricot glaze, then cover background with dark brown. Cover rest of cake with glaze.

Build up 2 rounded shapes for legs from pink sugarpaste and stick to rabbit body. Roll out pink icing and drape it over rabbit body. Trim away icing and smooth down over ears and legs. Roll a white scrap of sugarpaste into a ball for the eye and two strips for teeth. Moisten and stick in place. Colour scraps of sugarpaste dark pink and roll into eyelashes, pupil and oval shapes for ears. Moisten and position. Make a brown nose.

Roll marbled light brown sugarpaste into strips and cover the top and sides of hutch. Cover the strip across front of hutch as shown. Mark with a ruler to represent the wooden planks. Mark on nails with a brown food colouring pen. Position marshmallow for rabbit's tail.

To make lettuces, roll out green sugarpaste thinly and cut into small rounds. Flute up edges by rolling a wooden cocktail stick back and forth over them. Moisten and stick to 2 corners of hutch. Make carrot tops from scraps of green sugarpaste. Roll a quarter of orange sugarpaste into 3 carrots. Dampen and stick in one corner with green tops. Roll yellow and orange sugarpaste into a ball, push through a garlic press to make straw for bottom of hutch. Use spaghetti for whiskers.

*Serves 8-10.*

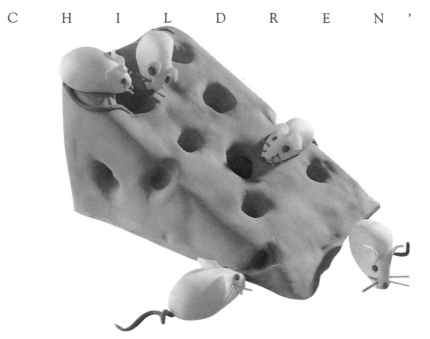

# ──────── NAUGHTY MICE ────────

one quantity of 4-egg Victoria Sponge mixture, baked
   in a 900 g (2lb) loaf tin at 160C (325F/Gas 3) for
   1¼ hours
30 cm (12 in) square cake board
FOR THE DECORATION:
6 tablespoons apricot glaze (see page 10)
800 g (1¾ lb) sugarpaste ready-to-roll icing
yellow and pink paste food colourings
strands thin spaghetti

Trim cake and cut in half horizontally and
diagonally, then join 2 halves side by side,
with apricot glaze. Trim, then spoon out
holes with a teaspoon. Brush cake all over
with apricot glaze.

Place cake on board. Colour three quarters of
sugarpaste yellow and roll out thinly. Drape
the yellow sugarpaste loosely over cake and
press into hollows. Smooth down over cake,
shape corners, then trim away excess icing.

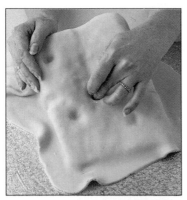

Using 25 g (1 oz) white sugar paste per mouse,
model 5 oval shapes for mouse bodies, then
mould thin ears. Stick on ears. Colour scraps
pink and roll into small balls for eyes and stick
on mice. Roll thin sausage shapes for tails.
Add spaghetti whiskers. Dampen mice and
position on cheese, then attach tails.

*Serves 8-10.*

# TORTOISE

one quantity of 4-egg Chocolate Victoria Sponge
    mixture, baked in a 3.3litre (6 pint/14 cup) pudding
    basin, measuring 25 cm (10 in) across the top, at
    160C (325F/Gas 3) for 1¼ hours
30 cm (12 in) round cake board
FOR THE DECORATION:
225 g (8 oz) chocolate butter cream (see page 10)
575 g (1¼ lb) chocolate-flavoured sugarpaste ready-
    to-roll icing
175 g (6 oz) sugarpaste ready-to-roll icing
black and green paste food colourings
115 g (4 oz) royal icing (see page 10)
55 g (2 oz) desiccated coconut and sugar flowers

Place cake upside down on board. Cut a large
groove for head and 4 small grooves for legs.

Spread all over with butter cream and smooth
down. Model a head and 4 legs from 115 g
(4 oz) chocolate sugarpaste, then roll out
remainder thinly. Make a cardboard template
from pattern on page 118 and cut round this
to make 28 hexagons. Stick hexagons, head
and legs onto body.

Make 2 white eyes from 25 g (1 oz) sugarpaste, then colour a scrap black for centres of
eyes. Colour royal icing, remaining sugarpaste and coconut green. Spread icing over
board, then sprinkle with coconut. To make
lettuce leaves, roll out green sugarpaste
thinly, cut out rounds then flute up edges by
rolling a wooden cocktail stick back and forth
over edges. Position leaves all round tortoise,
then decorate with flowers.

Serves 8.

# ——————— FARMYARD ———————

one quantity of 8-egg Victoria Sponge mixture, baked
in a 20 × 30 cm (8 × 12 in) oblong tin at 160C
(325F/Gas 3) for 1¼ hours
30 cm (12 in) square cake board
FOR THE DECORATION:
1 kg (2¼ lb) sugarpaste ready-to-roll icing
green, yellow, black, brown and cream paste food
colourings
6 tablespoons apricot glaze (see page 10)
55 g (2 oz) desiccated coconut
115 g (4 oz) royal icing (see page 10)

Cut a 5 cm (2 in) slice half the depth of the
cake from one end to make a ledge. Cut top
flat. Cut slice into 5 pieces.

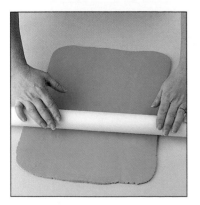

Colour 700 g (1½ lb) of the sugarpaste green.
Brush cake all over with apricot glaze. Roll
out green sugarpaste and cover cake. Smooth
down and trim edges.

Colour 55 g (2 oz) sugarpaste yellow. Brush cut pieces of cake with glaze, roll out yellow icing and cover to makes bales of straw. Prick ends with a skewer and mark on a straw effect. Place on cake. Make 5 bales.

To make sheep, roll 55 g (2 oz) white sugarpaste into 4 rolls. Mould heads, ears and legs. Stick heads on bodies.

Place white sugarpaste in a garlic press and press through to make woolly coats. Paint faces with black food colouring. Press wool onto sheep. Make 4.

To make cows, colour 55 g (2 oz) sugarpaste brown. Model as shown, make white horns, mouths and eyes and stick on. Colour some scraps black and make pupils for eyes. Flick bodies with a blunt cocktail stick to make fur. Make 3 or 4.

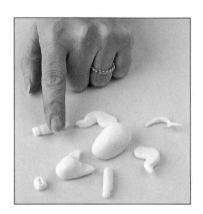

To make pigs, colour 115 g (4 oz) sugarpaste cream. Roll into bodies, heads, legs, tails and snouts as shown. Make 5.

Dampen pieces and pinch together. Use scraps of white and black sugarpaste to make eyes. Position eyes so that the pigs are looking in different directions.

Toast desiccated coconut until light brown. Colour royal icing green and brown. Spread icing onto cake to make a meadow and a pig-pen.

Sprinkle coconut over the pen. Stand the animals on the cake, then make fences with wooden cocktail sticks. Remove all the cocktail sticks before serving the cake.

*Serves 12-14.*

# CHIMPS' TEA PARTY

one quantity of 5-egg Victoria Sponge mixture, baked
  in a 20 cm (8 in) square tin at 160C (325F/Gas 3)
  for 1¼ hours
30 cm (12 in) square cake board
FOR THE DECORATION:
900 g (2 lb) sugarpaste ready-to-roll icing
6 tablespoons apricot glaze (see page 10)
cream, red, brown, pink, black and yellow paste food
  colourings
55 g (2 oz) royal icing (see page 10)
1 teaspoon caster sugar

Trim top of cake flat. Cut a 5 cm (2 in) slice
from cake and stick to centre with glaze to
form the table.

Colour 450 g (1 lb) sugarpaste cream, brush
cake all over with glaze and cover the cake.
Smooth down and trim sides.

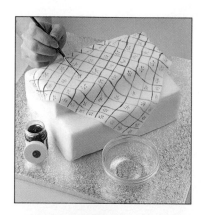

Roll out 115 g (4 oz) white sugarpaste into a 23 cm (9 in) square. Drape tablecloth over the table in the centre and paint on squares with red paste food colouring.

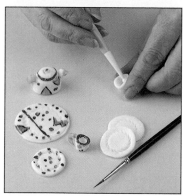

Make a teapot, cups and saucers from 55 g (2 oz) white sugarpaste. Paint on patterns with paste food colouring.

Model a cake, bread, buns and small cakes from scraps. Leave to dry, then paint as shown with food colouring.

To make chimps, colour 225 g (8 oz) sugar paste brown, 25 g (1 oz) beige and 25 g (1 oz) black. Roll into body pieces, arms, legs, ears and tails as shown. Make beige mouths and cut across. Roll 25 g (1 oz) into white balls for eyes and then dot with smaller black balls. Assemble as shown.

Dampen pieces, then stick chimp's arms and legs onto body. Stick on tail, then head. Make 6 chimps.

Position chimps round sides of cake and at the table as shown. Place arms in different positions.

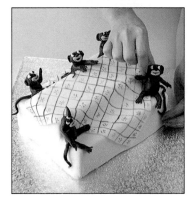

Place the food, cups and saucers on the table in a haphazard way and stick down with a little royal icing.

Colour remaining royal icing light brown and paint on the tablecloth for spilt tea as shown. Add sugar spilling out of the sugarbowl.

*Serves 12.*

# JUNGLE FEVER

one quantity of 5-egg Victoria Sponge mixture, baked in a 20 cm (8 in) square tin at 160C (325F/Gas 3) for 1¼ hours

30 cm (12 in) square cake board

FOR THE DECORATION:

4 tablespoons apricot glaze (see page 10)

1.35 kg (3 lb) sugarpaste ready-to-roll icing

green, brown, orange, blue, yellow, red, grey, pink and black paste food colourings

Trim cake flat, turn upside down and place on cake board. Brush with apricot glaze. Colour 750 g (1 lb 10 oz) sugarpaste bright green. Roll out, cover cake, smooth and trim. Keep trimmings wrapped in plastic wrap.

Colour remaining sugarpaste as follows: 115 g (4 oz) dark green, 115 g (4 oz) khaki green, 100 g (3½ oz) dark brown, 15 g (½ oz) light brown, 45 g (1½ oz) light orange, 25 g (1 oz) dark orange, 25 g (1 oz) pale blue, 25 g (1 oz) yellow, 7 g (¼ oz) red, 85 g (3 oz) grey, 15 g (½ oz) pink, 15 g (½ oz) black, leave rest white. Keep all pieces tightly wrapped in plastic wrap.

To make monkey and bears, flatten out dark brown sugarpaste into a round and mould ears. Mould light brown lips and muzzles and stick on. Mark with a knife and a skewer.

Add white circles for eyes, then black dots. Mould arms, hands and tail from brown scraps.

To make lion, mould light orange sugarpaste into a pear shape, moulding out 2 ears. Push dark orange sugarpaste through a garlic press and stick on for mane. Add white circles for eyes and mark on mouth with very thin black paste. Add a brown nose.

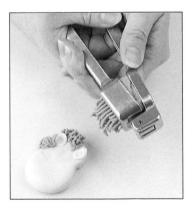

To make elephant, mould grey sugarpaste into an oval and pull the base into a trunk. Mould 2 big ears. Flatten out pink paste and fill in ears. Make eyes from white circles of sugarpaste, then top with black dots. Mark trunk.

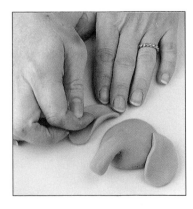

To make parrot, mould blue sugarpaste into a half moon shape. Make a smaller wing shape from a thinner piece of blue sugarpaste.

Roll red, yellow and orange sugarpaste into thin strips and stick to body and wings. Snip into feathers with small scissors. Make an orange beak and a black and white eye as shown.

To make snake, roll a long thin sausage of yellow sugarpaste and flatten out top into a head. Snip into 2 jaws. Make black and white eyes from small balls and a red tongue. Paint body with red food colouring.

Roll out dark, light and khaki green sugarpastes. Cut into long thin leaves. Moisten animals lightly with a little water and press onto covered cake. Moisten leaves and interleave in varying tones of green between the animals, curling and bending them haphazardly.

*Serves 8-10.*

# NOAH'S ARK

one quantity of 5-egg Victoria Sponge mixture, baked
in a 20 cm (8 in) square tin at 160C (325F/Gas 3)
for 1¼ hours
30 cm (12 in) square cake board
FOR THE DECORATION:
8 tablespoons apricot glaze (see page 10)
1.4 kg (3 lb 2 oz) sugarpaste ready-to-roll icing
green, black, red, blue and beige paste food colourings

Cut cake down the middle into 2 oblongs.
Trim one into a boat shape as shown. Keep 2
triangular end pieces. Cut other oblong into a
block and position triangles to make a sloping
roof as shown. Brush pieces with apricot
glaze.

Colour sugarpaste as follows: 475 g (1 lb 2 oz)
dark green, 400 g (14 oz) light green, 55 g
(2 oz) black, 350 g (12 oz) red, 25 g (1 oz)
blue, 25 g (1 oz) beige, 45 g (1½ oz) grey and
leave 15 g (½ oz) white. Roll out dark green
sugarpaste into an oblong, make 4 cuts from
the corners in towards the centre and cover
base of boat. Smooth over and trim. Roll out
blue sugarpaste and stamp out circles, then
stick them onto boat.

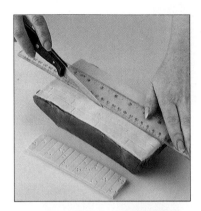

Roll out beige sugarpaste and cover top of boat. Mark on wooden planks with a sharp knife. Roll beige scraps to an oblong 15 × 4 cm (6 × 1½ in) for the gangplank. Place it on a strip of cardboard the same size, mark with a knife and leave to dry out.

Cover walls of cabin light green. Roll out black sugarpaste and make a door and 4 windows. Stick onto the green sugarpaste.

Position house on the boat part. Roll out red sugarpaste and cover the roof. Mark on tiles with a sharp knife. Make a small square chimney. Place 2 black rounds on top, then fit onto roof.

Roll out beige, white and grey sugarpaste thickly. Cut out 2 elephants, 2 giraffes, 2 kangaroos and 2 zebras from templates (opposite). Paint as shown. Leave to dry out for 3 hours until stiff, then place round the ark. Stick gangplank in position.

*Serves 8.*

GIRAFFE

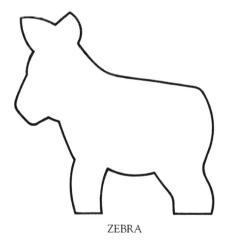

KANGAROO

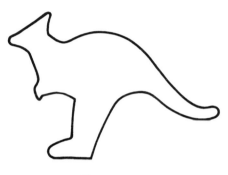

ZEBRA

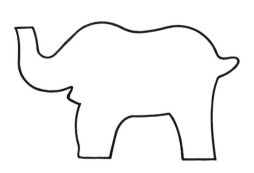

ELEPHANT

# ──────TEDDY BEARS' PICNIC──────

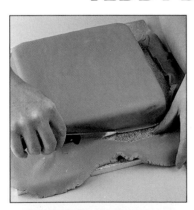

one quantity of 5-egg Victoria Sponge mixture, baked
  in a 20 cm (8 in) square tin at 160C (325F/Gas 3)
  for 1¼ hours
30 cm (12 in) square cake board
FOR THE DECORATION:
5 tablespoons apricot glaze (see page 10)
1.25 kg (2¾ lb) sugarpaste ready-to-roll icing
green, red, blue, cream, beige and yellow paste food
  colourings
225 g (8 oz) royal icing (see page 10)

Trim top of cake flat and place on cake board.
Brush top and sides of cake with apricot glaze.
Colour 900 g (2 lb) sugarpaste green, roll out
to a square and cover cake. Smooth and trim.

Re-roll scraps into strips wide enough to
cover cake board. Dab on a little royal icing
and stick down. Mark on a pattern all over
green icing with the tines of a fork to represent grass. Colour 175 g (6 oz) sugarpaste
pink, then roll out to a thin 20 cm (8 in)
square. Make small cuts into edges with
needlework scissors to make a fringe.
Dampen and place mat centrally on cake.
Mark on a dotted pattern with a skewer.

Model small plates, cups and a teapot from 55 g (2 oz) white sugarpaste. Paint with blue food colouring. Model scraps into bread, sandwiches and tarts as shown. Paint with red and cream food colouring. Leave to dry out for 2 hours. Make a bottle of drink from a scrap of green sugarpaste.

To make teddies, colour 150 g (5 oz) icing beige. Shape into an oval 2.5 cm (1 in) long. Shape head and pinch front to shape snout. Add 2 small ears. Shape arms and legs. Roll out 2 balls of white for eyes. Make 3 black rounds, place 2 in centre of eyes and one for nose. Dampen all pieces and stick together, then position on cake to dry. Mould 3 large bears and 3 smaller ones.

Decorate sides of cake with sugarpaste flowers and royal icing coloured dark green and piped on to represent leaves and stalks.

Place food and china on the mat, and stick on with plain royal icing. Place bears in position and stick on with small dabs plain royal icing.

*Serves 8-10.*

## CIRCUS

one quantity of 4-egg Victoria Sponge mixture, baked
   in two 20 cm (8 in) sandwich tins at 180C
   (350F/Gas 4) for 30 minutes
30 cm (12 in) round cake board
FOR THE DECORATION:
8 tablespoons apricot glaze (see page 10)
950 g (2 lb 2 oz) sugarpaste ready-to-roll icing
yellow, red, black, green, blue and orange paste food
   colourings
225 g (8 oz) royal icing (see page 10)
115 g (4 oz) caster sugar
small red and white striped candles
piece florist's wire and black edible food marker pen

Sandwich cakes together with apricot glaze
and cover sides with glaze.

Colour 350 g (12 oz) sugarpaste yellow, 350 g
(12 oz) red, 115 g (4 oz) black, 25 g (1 oz)
green, 25 g (1 oz) dark blue, 25 g (1 oz)
orange, 25 g (1 oz) light blue. Roll out yellow
sugarpaste to a long narrow strip. Roll up into
a coil and press round sides of cake. Place
cake on cake board.

Colour royal icing light orange and spread all over top of cake with a palette knife. Colour caster sugar light orange to represent sand, and sprinkle half of it over the royal icing. Leave to dry out for 1 hour, then add remaining sugar, brushing into a swirling pattern.

Roll out red sugarpaste thinly. Cut into 5 crescent shapes as shown. Pinch into 2 sections to represent fabric. Lightly dampen sides of cake with water and press red sugarpaste on as shown. Press in candles all round sides of circus ring.

To make seals, model black sugarpaste into an oblong with a pointed end. Mould 2 flippers and snip tail into sections with scissors, then mould flat. Mark with a wooden cocktail stick. Make 2 seals, then model 4 balls from orange and green sugarpaste. Thread onto wire and position between seals' heads. Make tiny balls from white icing for eyes and place black sugarpaste pupils in centre. Make 2.

To make clowns, make a round coloured ball for the body, then roll different coloured sugarpaste into sausage shapes for arms and legs. Make a frill for neck by fluting out a tiny round with a wooden cocktail stick. Make buttons and a round red rose. Make a white head, pointed hat and pompons. Paint on eyes and mouth with black food marker. Make hair by pressing orange and yellow sugarpaste through a garlic press. Dampen pieces and assemble as shown. Make 2.

*Serves 8.*

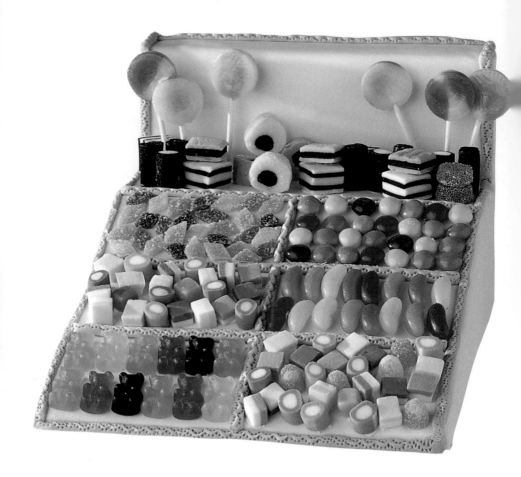

# SWEETSHOP

one quantity of 5-egg Victoria Sponge mixture, baked
   in a 20 cm (8 in) square, deep cake tin at 160C
   (325F/Gas 3) for 1¾ hours, cooled and half frozen
35 × 30 cm (14 × 12 in) oblong cake board
FOR THE DECORATION:
8 tablespoons apricot glaze (see page 10)
1.35 kg (3 lb) sugarpaste ready-to-roll icing
peach, yellow and blue paste food colourings
selection of sweets and lollipops
55 g (2 oz) royal icing (see page 10)

Cut away a 2.5 cm (1 in) wide strip from cake
and reserve.

Measure 4 cm (1½ in) in from cut edge of
cake and cut away a sloping piece as shown.

Place on cake board. Cut reserved strip in half crosswise and position the 2 pieces on the flat part of the cake (this will be the back of shop). Position the cut off slope in front of the cake as shown and stick together with glaze. Completely cover cake with apricot glaze.

Colour 575 g (1¼ lb) sugarpaste peach, 575 g (1¼ lb) lemon and 225 g (8 oz) light blue. Roll out peach sugarpaste to an oblong and cover centre panel of cake.

Roll out yellow sugarpaste and cover back and sides. Roll blue sugarpaste into long thin sausages. Moisten with water and crimp onto cake as shown, making 6 partitions.

Fill each section with sweets and stick down with a dab of royal icing. Decorate back section with liquorice sweets and lollipops.

*Serves 12.*

**Note:** Half freezing the cake makes it easier to cut.

# ——PUNCH & JUDY SHOW——

one quantity of 8-egg Victoria Sponge mixture, baked
  in a 20 × 30 cm (8 × 12 in) cake tin at 160C
  (325F/Gas 3) for 1¼ hours
30 cm (12 in) square cake board
FOR THE DECORATION:
900 g (2 lb) sugarpaste ready-to-roll icing
red, brown, yellow, pink, blue, green, black and orange
  paste food colourings
6 tablespoons apricot glaze (see page 10)

Cut an oblong out of the top of cake for
the stage.

Colour 115 g (4 oz) sugarpaste brown. Roll
out into a square for the stage background.
Dampen and stick down.

Colour 225 g (8 oz) sugarpaste red and 225 g (8 oz) yellow. Roll into long thin strips. Cover cake with glaze. Position strips on the cake as shown to form a stage with curtains.

For the puppets, colour 55 g (2 oz) sugarpaste flesh pink, 55 g (2 oz) brown, 55 g (2 oz) blue, 55 g (2 oz) green, 25 g (1 oz) black. Copy the templates on page 119 onto cardboard. To make Mr Punch, cut out the head with a hooked nose and 2 hands from pink sugarpaste. Make a red hat.

To make Mr Punch's body twist red and yellow strips together, then roll out and cut out. Make a frill from white scraps by fluting up a small round of white sugarpaste with a wooden cocktail stick. Paint on face as shown.

To make Mrs Punch, cut out a blue body and dress, flesh-coloured face and hand and make a mob-cap from a scrap of white sugarpaste rolled into a circle, then frilled up with a toothpick. Paint on face and make a red tongue. Assemble as shown. Roll out a small piece of brown sugarpaste to make a rolling pin, and place in her hand.

To make baby, roll a small ball of flesh-coloured sugarpaste for the head and an oval for the body, then roll up in a square of white sugarpaste. Roll 2 sausage shapes for arms. Paint on face.

To make crocodile, cut out 2 jaws from green sugarpaste and make teeth from white scraps. Position eye as shown.

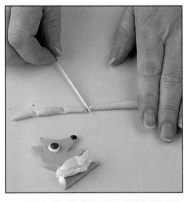

To make dog, colour scraps light brown and cut out shape as shown, then position on features. Make ruff from white scraps. To make sausages, roll pink sugarpaste into a long strip and pinch into sausages. Position sausages in dog's mouth and hang them over side of stage.

Cut out top piece for stage from 55 g (2 oz) orange sugarpaste. Position, then mark as shown with a skewer.

*Serves 12-14.*

# ——— GINGERBREAD HOUSE ———

FOR THE BISCUIT BASE:
3 tablespoons golden syrup
175 g (6 oz) butter
175 g (6 oz) soft dark brown sugar
700 g (1½ lb) plain flour
1½ teaspoons bicarbonate of soda
2 teaspoons ground ginger
1 teaspoon mixed spice
½ teaspoon ground cinnamon
9-10 tablespoons milk
3 egg yolks, beaten
35 cm (14 in) square cake board
FOR THE DECORATION:
1 kg (2¼ lb) royal icing (see page 10)
coloured sweets

Preheat the oven to 180C (350F/Gas 4).
Line 4 baking sheets with non-stick or
silicone paper. Transfer the templates on
page 99 onto graph paper and then trace onto
stiff card. In a saucepan, melt golden syrup,
butter and sugar over a gentle heat. Remove
from heat and cool. Sift flour, soda and spices
into a bowl and make a well. Pour in melted
mixture, milk and egg. Knead to a soft,
smooth dough.

Roll out warm dough between 2 sheets of silicone paper. Lift away top sheet. Leave rolled out dough on bottom sheet and cut round templates. Lift away excess dough and re-roll. Bake in the oven for 10 minutes until golden. While still hot, place template on hot biscuit and check shape. Cut round template to remove any dough that has spread on baking. Work while dough is still warm, it will become hard and brittle as it cools.

Leave the pieces to cool and harden flat on the baking sheets, then peel away paper. Leave flat for 5 hours to become completely firm. To assemble, take the 4 walls and pipe royal icing along base and side edges. Stand them together on cake board and leave to dry out for 1 hour until firm.

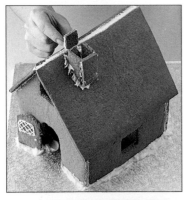

Stick on roof pieces with royal icing, and leave to dry and firm. Stick on the doors and shutters, and make the chimney from the 4 sloping pieces.

Decorate the roof and shutters with piped royal icing as shown. Stick on colourful sweets. Flick royal icing over the roof for a snowy effect.

*Serves 12-14.*

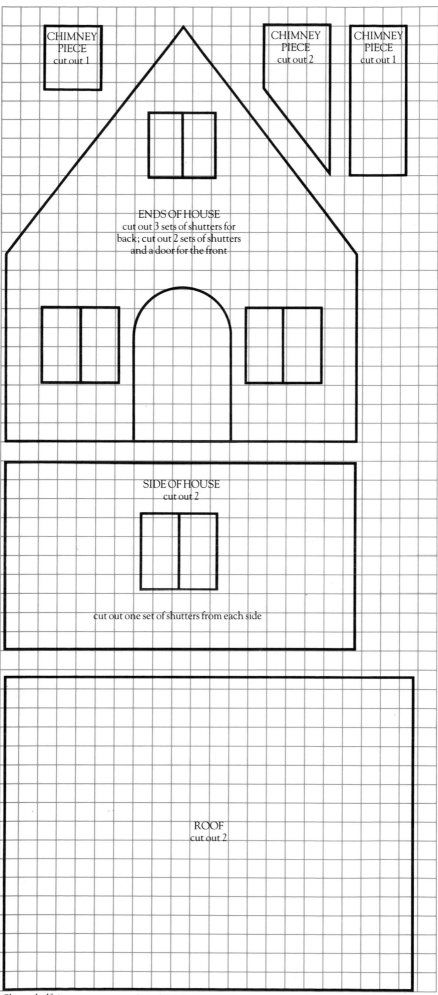

CHIMNEY PIECE
cut out 1

CHIMNEY PIECE
cut out 2

CHIMNEY PIECE
cut out 1

ENDS OF HOUSE
cut out 3 sets of shutters for
back; cut out 2 sets of shutters
and a door for the front

SIDE OF HOUSE
cut out 2

cut out one set of shutters from each side

ROOF
cut out 2

Shown half size – one square = 1 cm (½ in)

# FAIRY CASTLE

one quantity of 5-egg Victoria Sponge mixture, baked
  in a 20 cm (8 in) square cake tin at 160C (325F/
  Gas 3) for 1¼ hours and one quantity of 4-egg
  mixture, baked in two 20 cm (8 in) sandwich tins at
  180C (350F/Gas 4) for 30 minutes
4 mini swiss rolls and 4 ice cream cones
35 cm (14 in) square cake board
FOR THE DECORATION:
9 tablespoons apricot glaze (see page 10)
1 kg (2¼ lb) sugarpaste ready-to-roll icing
pink paste food colouring
225 g (8 oz) royal icing (see page 10)
225 g (8 oz) sugar, 21 sugar cubes and sugar flowers

Sandwich round cakes with glaze, place
on trimmed square cake and cut out wedge.

Carve cut piece into steps. Colour 900 g
(2 lb) sugarpaste shell pink. Brush the 4 swiss
rolls with glaze. Roll out the sugarpaste and
cover the rolls. Brush cakes with glaze. Roll
out remaining pink sugarpaste and drape over
cakes. Press down, trim and smooth over.
Cover steps with white sugarpaste and place
in position.

Mark a brickwork pattern onto the cake using a ruler and small knife. Mark all the walls.

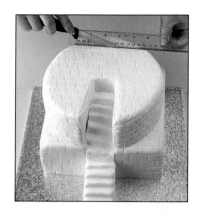

Attach the 4 swiss rolls to corners of square cake. Use wooden cocktail sticks to secure them to the cake, but remember to remove these when serving. Make 4 long windows from rolled out white sugarpaste. Moisten and attach.

Colour half the royal icing pink and spread over ice cream cones. Colour granulated sugar pink and spread on greaseproof paper. Roll the cones in the sugar to cover them.

Attach the cones to the towers, stick sugar cubes on top of round cake. Decorate windows and towers with flowers and piping as shown.

*Serves 14-16.*

# ─── TREASURE ISLAND ───

one quantity of 8-egg Victoria Sponge mixture, baked
 in a 30 × 20 cm (12 × 8 in) cake tin at 160C
 (325F/Gas 3) for 1¼ hours
35 cm (14 in) square cake board
FOR THE DECORATION:
225 g (8 oz) sugarpaste ready-to-roll icing
green, lilac, yellow, blue and brown paste food
 colourings
2 tablespoons apricot glaze (see page 10)
1 kg (2¼ lb) butter cream (see page 10)
225 g (8 oz) royal icing (see page 10)
115 g (4 oz) granulated sugar

Make palm leaves. Colour half sugarpaste
green, roll out and stamp out 5 circles with a
4 cm (1½ in) fluted cutter. Cut as shown.

Line a bun tin with plastic wrap and leave
fronds to dry out in a curved shape for 4
hours. Cut away corners of cake and cut into
the shape shown, sloping edges for sea shore.
Keep cut pieces to build up mountains in
centre of island.

Place cake on cake board. Coat cut pieces with apricot glaze and stick on in centre of island to make mountains. Colour 225 g (8 oz) butter cream lilac and spread over the hills.

Colour three 225 g (8 oz) batches of butter cream green, yellow and blue and 115 g (4 oz) cream. Spread green butter cream at foot of mountains to make grassy meadows. Spread cream icing for cliffs.

Spread yellow butter cream at foot of grass to make beaches and then spread blue icing on cake board for the sea. Colour granulated sugar yellow and sprinkle over for sand.

Colour 75 g (3 oz) of remaining sugarpaste brown and make trunks for palm trees. Stick green palm trees into grassy areas. Make a small treasure chest and map from remaining sugarpaste and decorate as shown.

*Serves 12-14.*

**Note:** Fill chest with gold foil and your own choice of sweets.

# LITTLE MERMAIDS

one quantity of 5-egg Victoria Sponge mixture, baked
   in a 20 cm (8 in) square cake tin at 160C (325F/
   Gas 3) for 1¼ hours
30 cm (12 in) square cake board
FOR THE DECORATION:
1.25 kg (2¾ lb) sugarpaste ready-to-roll icing
blue, green, pink and yellow paste food colourings
6 tablespoons apricot glaze (see page 10)

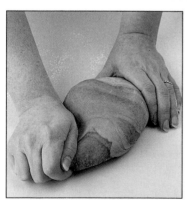

Colour 350 g (12 oz) sugarpaste a mottled
blue by only half kneading in the colouring.
Trim cake flat, spread with apricot glaze and
roll out sugarpaste to a square large enough to
cover top and sides of cake. Smooth down
and trim away excess sugarpaste.

Colour 115 g (4 oz) sugarpaste dark green and
115 g (4 oz) light green. Cut out into seaweed
shapes as shown. Dampen shapes and stick
round sides of cake, alternating dark and light
green colours.

To make mermaids, colour 225 g (8 oz) flesh pink and make head, arms and body as shown. Model a face and paint on eyes and lips with neat paste food colouring.

Stick mermaid's tops to cake. Colour 115 g (4 oz) sugarpaste yellow. Press through a garlic press and make long strands for hair. Dampen the heads with water and stick on the hair.

Colour 225 g (8 oz) sugarpaste a mottled turquoise blue/green. Roll out and stamp out small circles. Build up the centre of the tail with scraps. Mark each fish scale with a wooden cocktail stick and place on the tail, overlapping as shown. Place 2 white scalloped circles on the mermaid's top and paint with red food colouring.

Colour 115 g (4 oz) sugarpaste orange and make starfish, then make fish and pebbles from scraps and position as shown.

*Serves 8-10.*

## ROCK GUITAR

two quantities of 5-egg Victoria Sponge mixture, baked
   in two 20 cm (8 in) square tins at 160C (325F/
   Gas 3) for 1¼ hours
40 × 35 cm (16 × 14 in) oblong cake board
FOR THE DECORATION:
115 g (4 oz) butter cream (see page 10)
1 kg (2¼ lb) sugarpaste ready-to-roll icing
red, black, cream and blue paste food colourings
chocolate mint sticks
6 red sweets
red bootlace liquorice

Place cakes side by side and trim tops to level
them. Cut out guitar shape following diagram
on page 118.

Place pieces on cake board and stick together
with butter cream. Spread the cakes all over
with butter cream.

Colour three quarters of sugarpaste red, roll out thinly and drape over base of guitar. Trim away edges and smooth down.

Colour half remaining sugarpaste black and half cream. Roll out black sugarpaste and cut out a fingerboard shape, dampen and stick in position. Roll cream sugarpaste into a thin strip, dampen and cover the fingerboard. Roll into a coil and press round sides and over the neck, as shown.

Cut chocolate sticks in half and place on fingerboard to form struts.

Position long strips of red liquorice for guitar strings. Colour scraps of sugarpaste blue. Cut out tiny stars from blue and white sugarpaste. Decorate guitar with sweets and stars and white dots either end of guitar strings.

*Serves 12.*

**Variation:** Instead of liquorice, pipe the strings with royal icing.

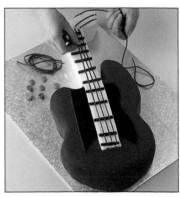

# FOOTBALL

two quantities of 2-egg Victoria Sponge mixture, baked
   in two 1 litre (35 floz/4½ cup) pudding basins at
   160C (325F/Gas 3) for 45 minutes
20 cm (8 in) round cake board
FOR THE DECORATION:
6 tablespoons apricot glaze (see page 10)
800 g (1¾ lb) sugarpaste ready-to-roll icing
115 g (4 oz) royal icing (see page 10)
55 g (2 oz) desiccated coconut
green and blue paste food colourings

Trim tops of cakes flat and stick together with
apricot glaze, securing with 2 wooden cocktail sticks (make sure you remove these when
serving). Trim cake to make a round.

Brush cake all over with apricot glaze. Roll
out 450 g (1 lb) white sugarpaste thinly.
Drape icing over cake and wrap it completely.
Trim away edges, then smooth all over.
Colour royal icing and desiccated coconut
green. Cover cake board with royal icing and
sprinkle coconut over it.

Colour 115 g (4 oz) sugarpaste dark blue. Roll
out blue sugarpaste and remaining white
sugarpaste. Cut out hexagon template using
pattern on page 118. Cut round template to
make blue and white hexagons, then stick
them on the football. Press or stretch hexagons in place if they don't fit exactly.

Serves 6-8.

**Variation:** Make a rosette from scraps of
sugarpaste, choosing the colours of your
favourite team.

# PAINTING PALETTE

one quantity of 6-egg Victoria Sponge mixture, baked
   in a 20 × 30 cm (8 × 12 in) cake tin at 160C
   (325F/Gas 3) for 1¼ hours
35 × 30 cm (14 × 12 in) oblong cake board
FOR THE DECORATION:
225 g (8 oz) butter cream (see page 10)
brown, red, black, blue, yellow, green and orange paste
   food colourings and edible silver food colouring
450 g (1 lb) sugarpaste ready-to-roll icing
225 g (8 oz) royal icing (see page 10)

Cut across top of cake so that it is flat. Cut
away the 4 corners, a curved base piece and
stamp out a 4 cm (1½ in) circle.

Spread butter cream over top and sides of
cake and place on cake board. Add brown
paste colouring to the sugarpaste and knead
in until a marbled effect is achieved. Roll out
and drape over cake, trim, then smooth over
with your palms.

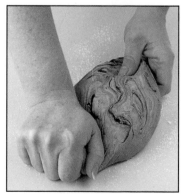

Re-roll sugarpaste scraps and colour red,
black and brown. Roll 55 g (2 oz) red and 25 g
(1 oz) black sugarpaste into thin sausages
and then into paintbrush shapes. Make brush
tops from brown sugarpaste and mark as
shown. Colour teaspoons of royal icing with
bright colours and spread on the palette with
a palette knife. Add the brushes. Paint brush
trims with silver food colouring.

*Serves 12.*

# BALLET SHOES

one quantity of 5-egg Victoria Sponge mixture, baked
  in a 20 cm (8 in) square cake tin at 160C
  (325F/Gas 3) for 1¼ hours
30 cm (12 in) square cake board
FOR THE DECORATION:
4 tablespoons apricot glaze (see page 10)
800 g (1¾ lb) sugarpaste ready-to-roll icing
pink paste food colouring

Cut cake in half down the middle. Carve
round each piece to make a pointed toe end
and a curved back to the shoe as shown.

Hollow out centres as shown. Brush all over
with apricot glaze. Colour three quarters of
sugarpaste shell pink. Mould a little sugarpaste into long sausages and make a ridge on
top of shoe and round the ends of the toes to
make the points.

Halve remaining pink sugarpaste and roll out each half into a horseshoe shape and a sole. Drape larger piece round each shoe and smooth over, pleating underneath the shoe. Stick sole on. Smooth all over the shoes using the palms of your hands. Stand the shoes on their points to make the flat blocked points.

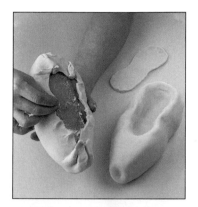

Roll out remaining white sugarpaste thinly and cut into 2 figure-of-eight shapes. Dampen inside of shoes and press white lining inside. Trim away any excess.

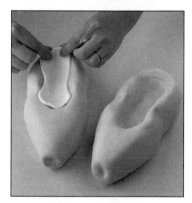

Using fingers or crimpers, crimp or mould top edges to make the binding. Mould round the toes. Make very thin sausages from scraps of sugarpaste and form into bows. Press on to front of shoes.

Roll out pink scraps to a long thin strip. Using a pastry wheel, cut 4 long, thin strips for the ribbons, dampen ends and attach ribbons to back of shoes. Drape ribbons across shoes.

*Serves 10.*

**Variation:** Instead of making the ribbons, use 1 metre (1 yd) of bought pink satin ribbon.

# ROLLER SKATES

one quantity of 5-egg Victoria Sponge mixture, baked
in a 20 cm (8 in) square tin at 160C (325F/Gas 3)
for 1¼ hours
35 cm (14 in) square cake board
½ bought swiss roll
FOR THE DECORATION:
450 g (1 lb) butter cream (see page 10)
225 g (8 oz) almond paste
1.75 kg (3¾ lb) sugarpaste ready-to-roll icing
green, black, red, yellow paste food colourings
5 mini swiss rolls
red bootlace liquorice and jelly sweets

Cut top of cake completely level, then cut
down middle to make 2 oblongs. Cut each
oblong into a sole shape as shown.

Cut the piece of swiss roll in half. Spread
butter cream over top of cakes and stick swiss
roll onto the oblong, securing with wooden
cocktail sticks (remember to remove these
when you serve the cake). Carve the cake for
toe piece as shown, and build up the gaps
with almond paste and spare pieces of cake.

Cover each cake with butter cream. Colour 900 g (2 lb) sugarpaste green and halve. Roll out each half thinly and drape over each shoe. Mould to a boot shape, trimming where necessary. Colour 350 g (12 oz) sugarpaste black and roll out thinly.

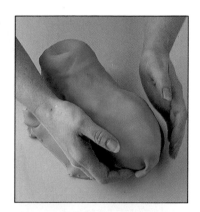

Press black sugarpaste onto sole piece on base of boots and up round sides of shoe. Pinch or crimp to make sharp edges. Mark a pattern on with a skewer to represent rubber. Colour 450 g (1 lb) icing yellow and roll out thinly to cover 4 mini swiss rolls for wheels. Cut remaining swiss roll in half and trim. Colour scraps red and cover halved mini swiss roll to make stops, then mark with a wooden cocktail stick.

Roll out green scraps to make a tongue and two tops for each boot. Make holes for shoelaces with a skewer, then fill holes with red bootlace liquorice for laces.

Place boots on cake board. Place wheels and stops in position. Cut out yellow and red stars, dampen and stick onto boots. Decorate wheels with jelly sweets. Place red scraps of sugarpaste in top of each boot.

*Serves 10.*

# CHESSBOARD

one quantity of 5-egg Victoria Sponge mixture, baked
 in a 20 cm (8 in) square tin at 160C
 (325F/Gas 3) for 1¼ hours
25 cm (10 in) square cake board
FOR THE DECORATION:
4 tablespoons apricot glaze (see page 10)
700 g (1½ lb) almond paste
800 g (1¾ lb) sugarpaste ready-to-roll icing
cream, red and black paste food colourings

Trim top of cake flat. Turn over and place on
cake board. Brush all over with apricot glaze.
Roll out almond paste and cover the top and
sides of cake. Pinch corners together to give
sharp edges. Leave to dry for 2 hours.

Colour half the sugarpaste cream, a quarter
red and leave a quarter white. Roll out half
the cream sugarpaste into a 20 × 10 cm (8 ×
4 in) oblong. Cut into four 2.5 cm (1 in) wide
strips, then divide each strip into 8, making
32 squares. Repeat with the red icing.

Lightly moisten top of cake with boiled water, then carefully stick the squares on top of the cake alternately. Cover whole top of cake with 32 red squares and 32 cream ones. Lightly roll over the surface with a rolling pin.

Roll out the remaining cream sugarpaste to 4 strips long and wide enough to cover the 4 sides of the cake. Dampen sides of the cake lightly, then stick on the cream strips. Smooth over until completely flat, then pinch or crimp the joins to make them square.

Re-roll red and cream trimmings into long thin sausages and twist together. Dampen slightly, then place along the top joins to decorate.

To make chessmen, colour half remaining sugarpaste black and leave other half white. Mould into chess pieces as shown. Leave to dry out for 2 hours and then stick lightly to squares on the board.

*Serves 12.*

**Note:** This cake needs to be covered with almond paste to start with, to give a flat surface on which to mount the squares.

# COMPUTER

one quantity of 3-egg Victoria Sponge mixture, baked
   in a 18 × 28 cm (7 × 11 in) cake tin at 180C
   (350F/Gas 4) for 30 minutes and two quantities of
   5-egg mixture, baked in two 20 cm (8 in) square tins
   at 160C (325F/Gas 3) for 1¼ hours
35 cm (14 in) square cake board
FOR THE DECORATION:
450 g (1 lb) butter cream (see page 10)
2 kg (4½ lb) sugarpaste ready-to-roll icing
black, cream, red, yellow, green and blue paste food
   colourings and black food colouring pen
long length black liquorice

Trim top of 18 × 28 cm (7 × 11 in) cake flat
and turn it over. Trim away front to a slope
as shown.

Cover top and sides thinly with butter cream.
Trim tops of 2 square cakes completely flat,
sandwich together with butter cream and cut
away a sloping piece as shown. Cover all sides
thinly with butter cream.

Colour half sugarpaste grey, a quarter black and remainder cream. Roll out grey sugarpaste thinly and cover keyboard and computer. Trim away edges and smooth over until completely flat. Pinch to neaten and make straight edges.

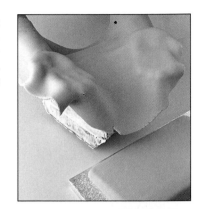

Roll out black sugarpaste to a 16 cm (6½ in) square for the screen. Dampen lightly then press onto computer body. Roll out about 85 g (3 oz) cream sugarpaste into a sausage, press round black screen to form a ridge as shown.

Roll out remaining cream sugarpaste to a rectangle and cut into 46 squares measuring about 2.5 cm (1 in), plus a long return bar and 2 rectangles either end. Dampen pieces and press onto keyboard, then using a food colouring pen, write on the letters and numerals. Use grey scraps to mould into a mouse.

Mark ridges on sides of keyboard and computer with a ruler. Make wire attachment from liquorice and join computer to keyboard and to mouse. Colour scraps red, yellow, green and blue. Cut into shapes to make a game picture on the screen.

*Serves 14-16.*

**Variation:** Use bought decorative birthday letters and numerals if you don't want to make your own keyboard.

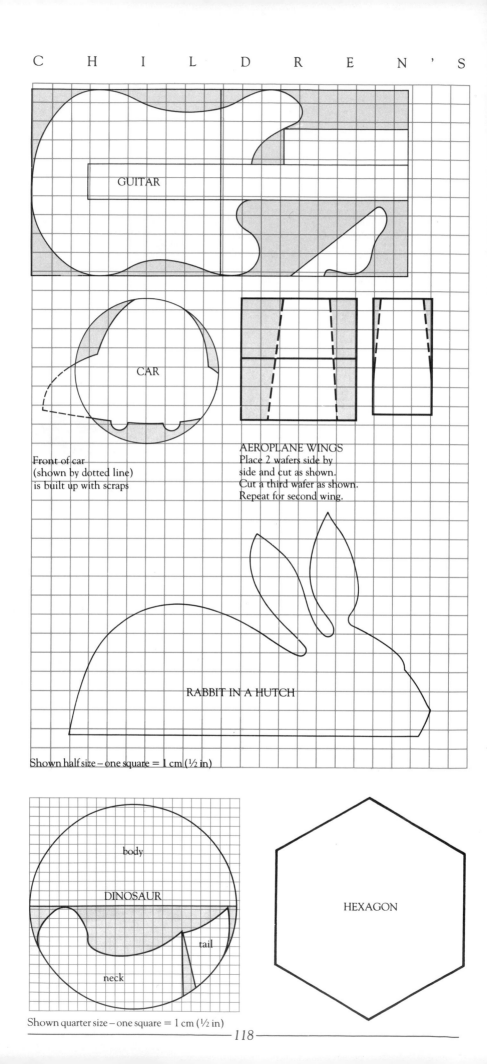

GUITAR

CAR

Front of car
(shown by dotted line)
is built up with scraps

AEROPLANE WINGS
Place 2 wafers side by
side and cut as shown.
Cut a third wafer as shown.
Repeat for second wing.

RABBIT IN A HUTCH

Shown half size – one square = 1 cm (½ in)

body

DINOSAUR

tail

neck

HEXAGON

Shown quarter size – one square = 1 cm (½ in)

TOP PIECE FOR STAGE

MRS PUNCH

DOG

MR PUNCH

CROCODILE

# INDEX